THE SUSTAINABLE HOUSE HANDBOOK

THE SUSTAINABLE HOUSE HANDBOOK

HOW TO PLAN AND BUILD AN
AFFORDABLE, ENERGY-EFFICIENT
AND WATERWISE HOME
FOR THE FUTURE

JOSH BYRNE

Hardie Grant

BOOKS

For Ollie and Caitlin,
and a low carbon future.

CONTENTS

FOREWORD

The Sustainable House Handbook should rightly be considered a valuable tool for anyone thinking about building a sustainable home. Josh Byrne has a unique background and has poured himself into this book, providing impeccable research, expert insight and considered explanations for each design element.

Josh's project began with a simple goal and an authentic approach, arrived at after years of working on the ideas. He set out to make a house that was affordable for most people and could not only minimise its energy and water use but make more renewable energy than it consumed. It also had to be visually pleasing and liveable for his young family and, of course, be integrated within a beautiful and hardworking garden good enough to go on national TV every Friday night.

The project has reach because of Josh's credentials as a globally significant researcher. He created a data management system with seventy channels monitoring the performance of the home and then worked with other researchers to interpret it. This included how an electric vehicle fitted into the household system. Analysing the research data – testing the house and testing the findings – told him whether it was truly working or not, and informed how he could make it work better. The results have been produced in academic journals and other books with all the research detail for the world to see.

Another impressive feature of the project is the open research available on the Josh's House website, which gets hundreds of thousands of hits every year. All the technical data and procedures of the design and findings have been provided there, so others can benefit from this valuable information.

I am considered to be an expert in sustainable cities and often get asked to speak on hopeful examples of where it is happening. I can dine out on Josh's House and its remarkable story anywhere in the world and have done so many times in the past few years. I can now also direct people to this book as a vivid demonstration of a successful sustainable home and the evidence behind it. I hope you will pass a copy of this beautiful book on to your grandchildren as it marks the time in history when we got serious about sustainability in our own homes.

Peter Newman AO
Professor of Sustainability Curtin University
and Coordinating Lead Author IPCC
(Intergovernmental Panel on Climate Change)

PREFACE

Over the years I've been fortunate to rent multiple homes where I've
been able to work on the garden and fix up the houses. This started
with my first rental at the age of eighteen. It was an old property in a
leafy Perth suburb which became my student house for the next six
years while studying at university. I took the lease on because the place
had a wonderful overgrown yard with lots of potential. My mates and
I landscaped the garden and even renovated some of the rooms in the
house. The owners lived overseas, so we just got on with it. In addition
to tackling the garden, we experimented with all sorts of DIY structures,
including outdoor living spaces and even converted an old Kombi into a
spare room. When I look back on it, my interest in sustainable housing
and design developed there.

After graduating, I travelled overseas, and on returning to Perth I rented
another house. Once again, it was an old place that needed some love.
By this stage I had started working as a presenter on ABC TV's *Gardening
Australia* so I had the opportunity to fix it up step-by-step 'on camera'
over time, learning as I went and sharing the stories along the way. Here,
I got more ambitious with building and fixing up the old house to make
it more comfortable as well as energy and water efficient, incorporating
rainwater harvesting, greywater reuse and building a studio. When this
place was done, I moved onto another rental project, and then another
several years after that. Both involved major landscaping and building
activities supported by the owners. I installed solar PV with their
permission, fixed draughty windows and doors, and most importantly
I made each house a home that was comfortable and efficient to run.
Two of the houses became case studies for my PhD. I learnt a lot and
enjoyed the challenge of new projects. It was also great material for TV.

When my partner Kellie and I started a family, we decided it was time
to get our own place and we liked the idea of starting from scratch
and building something new. We are both environmental scientists,
so it's no surprise that environmental performance was front of mind

> We would have a
> home that would look
> like many others up
> and down the street
> but perform very
> differently

when developing the brief, as was comfort and affordability. Thankfully, these objectives aren't mutually exclusive if the design and build are approached the right way.

Our first concept plan was a little more ambitious than what we eventually settled on. The design and layout are similar, but the building is a lot more 'normal' than what we originally envisaged. Our first concept incorporated walls made from rammed recycled building rubble, salvaged timbers and bespoke features. After getting the design costed, we soon realised that we were dreaming. The price was out of reach. But rather than changing our expectations on performance, comfort and efficiency, we rethought the look. What if we built a home made from more common construction materials, and engaged a regular builder who catered for the volume housing market? If we did this, while emphasising the importance of design, we would have a home that would look like many others up and down the street but perform very differently.

As our thinking about the building project matured, so did the idea of sharing our experience of building a high-performance home within a similar time frame and price range as a regular house. In addition to building the house, we made a commitment to document the journey through videos, monitor the operational performance and publish the results. For five years, the house was used as a 'living laboratory' in partnership with research institutions to test ideas and showcase the benefits of sustainable housing. To check out the material we published during this time, head to joshshouse.com.au, where you can also take a virtual tour of the house and garden to see how it all came together. The outcomes are clear – high-performance homes that are comfortable and healthy to live in, affordable to run and have good environmental outcomes are accessible and cost-effective. They don't have to be complicated or boutique, but it takes effort to get something better than 'the norm'. It's important to get informed and communicate expectations to the builder to get the best outcome. This handbook has been written to share the research and outcomes of our build – shaped by the lived experience of it as our family home – and is intended to be a useful resource to help people get the sustainable house that is right for them.

> The outcomes are clear – high-performance homes that are comfortable and healthy to live in, affordable to run and have good environmental outcomes are accessible and cost-effective

INTRODUCTION

For many of us, building a new home is one of the biggest projects we'll ever undertake. There's a lot to it, and it can be a stressful process. Knowing where to start is a challenge in itself, especially if you are looking for something a little bit different from the standard product on the market.

Building or renovating a home also presents a tangible opportunity to make a positive environmental contribution. Residential buildings account for around 10% of Australia's greenhouse gas emissions and, as demonstrated with our house, building houses that have a net-zero operational carbon footprint is readily achievable. Residential construction is also a major source of building waste, and homes and gardens have a high demand for water. These issues are easily dealt with through considered design and thoughtful construction, and it needn't mean sacrifice or exorbitant cost.

Research has shown that there is a growing interest in the idea of a sustainable home, not only for environmental reasons, but for personal benefits too. By unpacking this term and defining the core attributes of a sustainable house – energy and water efficient, comfortable, cost-effective to operate and healthy to live in – it's easy to see why this is appealing. More to the point, why aren't all houses built like this? The unfortunate reality is that they are not. Most new homes are built to minimum energy-efficiency compliance and, even then, sometimes fall short of the most basic benchmarks due to poor attention to detail in construction.

Knowing what to look for when choosing a site to build on, or what the best design response should be for the one you have, is the first step in creating a house that can perform to its potential. Having a clear set of goals or guiding principles that prioritise sustainability outcomes is also important.

Building a new home is one of the biggest projects we'll ever undertake

The format of this book is intended to be both instructional and inspirational. The chapters present a logical sequence of information spanning the planning, design and construction of my family home. This case study provides a working example of how sustainable design principles, good practices and new technologies can be applied to improve the outcome of a build. The ideas presented are supported with illustrations and photographs from our project, and breakout sections are used to provide additional information on how the concepts presented can be applied in other regions and contexts.

Chapter 1 sets up the importance of planning and goal setting, including establishing clear sustainability objectives for a project. Energy efficiency compliance requirements are explained, and a range of other sustainability considerations are identified through the example of the Housing Industry Association's (HIA) GreenSmart protocol. This multi-criteria framework provides robust guidance for improving the sustainability of a build. We used it for our project as a way of documenting the various initiatives and communicating priorities with our builder. A summarised version of our GreenSmart checklist is provided on page 172 and includes specific details on the practices we employed and products we used.

Chapter 2 explains the principles of climate-responsive design, how they informed the design of our house, and key considerations for other climate zones around Australia.

The influence of building material choice on house thermal performance, air quality and environmental impact is covered in Chapter 3.

Chapter 4 addresses how energy is used in a home and provides guidance on efficient options for heating and cooling, hot water supply, lighting and appliances. Meeting the energy needs of a home through photovoltaic (PV) systems and batteries is discussed in Chapter 5.

Chapter 6 presents an integrated approach to water management, starting with the selection of water-efficient fixtures and appliances, combined with the use of alternate water sources such as rainwater and greywater for reduced reliance on mains water supply.

The format of this book is intended to be both instructional and inspirational, spanning the planning, design and construction of my family home

Chapter 7 highlights the important role that landscaping plays for improved sustainability, from enhancing the thermal performance of the house through to systems for food production and composting.

Chapter 8 looks at performance verification and explains several critical tests that can be conducted during a build. This section of the book is intended to prompt owners at concept stage to think about testing during their build, as simple checks may reveal a weakness that can be difficult or more costly to remedy after the fact.

This chapter also provides some general advice about targeting data collection and ongoing monitoring for an average building project. By contrast, in the 'living laboratory' that is our house, we have around seventy channels of data acquisition. This includes sensors to record internal room temperature and humidity, as well as outside conditions, to understand the thermal performance of the building. We also monitor energy use at a circuit level, along with solar energy generation and battery supply. We meter all our water sources, as well as the energy required to run these systems.

The analysis and reporting of this data provides an important evidence base in support of the ideas presented in this book, with the results presented throughout the chapters to illustrate how just how comfortable and efficient a sustainable house can be.

CHAPTER 1

PLANNING & OBJECTIVES

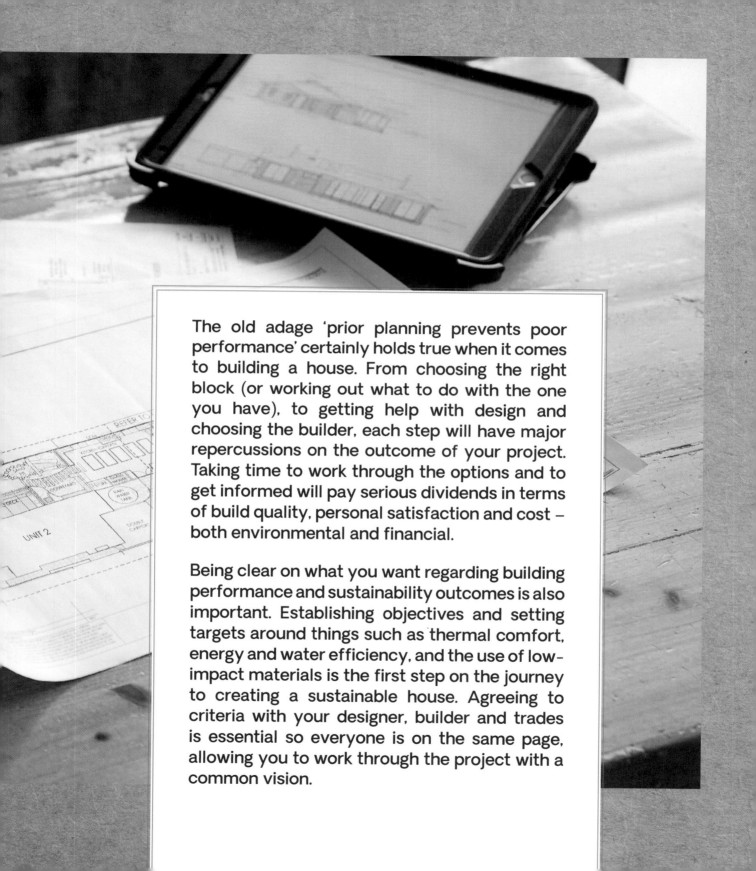

The old adage 'prior planning prevents poor performance' certainly holds true when it comes to building a house. From choosing the right block (or working out what to do with the one you have), to getting help with design and choosing the builder, each step will have major repercussions on the outcome of your project. Taking time to work through the options and to get informed will pay serious dividends in terms of build quality, personal satisfaction and cost – both environmental and financial.

Being clear on what you want regarding building performance and sustainability outcomes is also important. Establishing objectives and setting targets around things such as thermal comfort, energy and water efficiency, and the use of low-impact materials is the first step on the journey to creating a sustainable house. Agreeing to criteria with your designer, builder and trades is essential so everyone is on the same page, allowing you to work through the project with a common vision.

ABOVE: Regular site meetings with contractors ensured the building and landscaping processes went smoothly.
RIGHT: Slashing at the block to reduce fire risk and weed issues for neighbours prior to construction starting.

THE SITE

Choosing the right parcel of land to build on can be daunting. There's lots to consider. Location, neighbourhood, size and of course price all compete for importance when weighing up options. For us, finding a block with good solar access was at the top of the list, along with being in an established suburb with a strong sense of community. We were fortunate to find the perfect block to build on – a 1160 m² property in the Perth suburb of Hilton. It's only a short walk to the shops, the local park and public transport. Measuring around 60 m by 20 m on an east–west axis, the block was ideally suited to building a solar passive house (see Chapter 2). The location near the coast was a benefit due to cooling summer breezes.

We were fortunate to find the perfect block to build on – a 1160 m² property in the Perth suburb of Hilton

---

The site had a number of other things going for it – it was relatively flat, free draining and clear of any significant vegetation. The existing building was a very modest 1950s asbestos-clad cottage that wasn't suitable for retention. It needed to be deconstructed and useful materials salvaged. Other than the hazardous asbestos, which was professionally removed, the site was free from contamination and minimal site works were required. The only real issue was the cost. Buying the entire block on our own and building a house wasn't an option financially. Rather than letting the block go, we decided to partner with another family member to co-develop the site and build two houses – one for each of us.

This was a big decision. Other than mixing family and money, which is something that we are always advised to avoid, it meant that we'd need to allow additional time and costs for subdividing. It also meant that we'd have to navigate through design decisions that would impact on both parties and negotiate things like who gets which part of the block, and how to fairly divide the land. After careful consideration, we jointly agreed that all these things could be managed. To be honest, most things just fell into place. Lisa (my sister-in-law) wanted to build on the front of the property and face the street, while we wanted the privacy of the back. We both wanted our own separate access and private outdoor spaces but were also happy to have shared garden space. We agreed on finances and timing, as well as a set of guiding design principles that would inform how we would develop the property. With these fundamentals resolved, we purchased the block, and moved on to preparing the brief for how we would build our homes.

THE PLAN

For Kellie and me, designing and building a sustainable home was very important. We wanted a family home that would be comfortable year-round, without the need for air conditioning or additional heating. We wanted to produce adequate solar energy to meet household needs, at least on a net basis (where more energy is generated on site than is used in the home over a year), as well as be able to collect and recycle water and have a garden to provide food and for pleasure.

We were also mindful of designing the homes for accessibility so they could be used by people with mobility challenges, whether that be through age or injury (see Box on page 26, Universal Access Design).

Good indoor air quality through using non-toxic materials and adequate ventilation was important, as was the use of low-impact building materials that are durable and reusable or recyclable at the end of the building's life. These considerations also made good sense to Lisa and led to us engaging the same building designer, who specialised in solar passive homes, and eventually the same builder to construct both houses to bring efficiencies in logistics, cost and time to the process. Designing and building the houses together also allowed us to achieve a sense of cohesion across the property in terms of connecting spaces, materials and circulation.

The floor plans of both houses are typical of a family home – three bedrooms, two bathrooms and a laundry, with an open-plan kitchen, dining and living room area, plus an activities room that can function as a playroom or study, but there are a few important points of difference to most other houses. First, we wanted the homes to be compact in their design while still being roomy enough for a family. Second, we set the ambitious goal of achieving a 10-star rating under the Nationwide House Energy Rating Scheme (NatHERS) while using conventional building materials and construction methods to keep costs down.

The exterior design is a modern take on the classic Hilton brick-and-weatherboard look, with a mix of modern rendered finishes, old-style weatherboards and heritage red brickwork in high-impact areas. The sympathetic roof lines combined with the generous building setback of the front house fit comfortably with the 1950s feel of the suburb.

The property plan also presents a sensitive approach to residential subdivision that has maximised effective garden area around the homes to allow for good cross ventilation and natural shading, as well as for children's play spaces and food production – important health and lifestyle benefits that are rapidly disappearing from our suburbs.

To oversee the project, we decided I would project manage the build, coordinating with the designer and builder and directly with some of the trades. I strongly recommend that people get professional help for custom builds. Typically, this is the role of the architect and their role should be valued. Again, it's important that people choose the right one for them and that they understand the brief.

The Layout

The landscape at Josh's house has been designed to support multiple sustainability outcomes, including energy efficiency, water efficiency, waste reduction, biodiversity and food production, as well as providing lifestyle benefits.

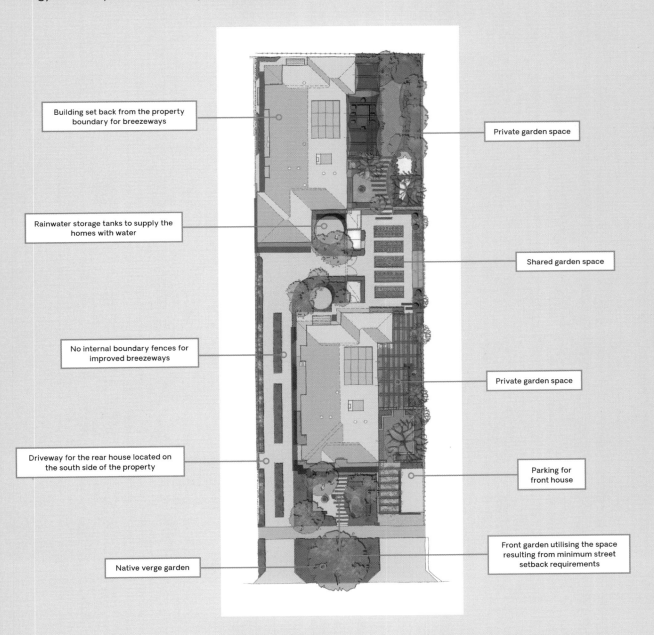

Building set back from the property boundary for breezeways

Private garden space

Rainwater storage tanks to supply the homes with water

Shared garden space

No internal boundary fences for improved breezeways

Private garden space

Driveway for the rear house located on the south side of the property

Parking for front house

Native verge garden

Front garden utilising the space resulting from minimum street setback requirements

The outdoor spaces were given equal priority to the houses during the planning and design process.

UNIVERSAL ACCESS DESIGN

Sustainable housing design needs to consider more than just environmental performance, it should also tackle issues such as social inclusiveness and design life. One way to address this is to incorporate universal access design principles to make homes accessible for people with mobility challenges. This is something that affects all of us, including families with young children, pregnant women, people who have a temporary or permanent injury or disability, and seniors. Key considerations to ensure universal access requirements are met include:

- Provide a flat, level walkway to the entrance with a 1000 mm minimum-width path and a 1200 mm × 1200 mm landing area to entrance door.

- Install a wide entrance doorway with 820 mm minimum clear width with a flush entry.

- Include wide internal doorways at 820 mm minimum and hallways at 1000 mm minimum.

- Provide at least one accessible toilet on the entry level with a 900 mm × 1200 mm space clear of a swinging door. If located in the bathroom, the toilet should be in the corner to enable the installation of grab rails.

- Provide at least one accessible shower on the entry level. The shower recess should be hobless (no step) and be in the corner of the room to enable the installation of grab rails.

- Provide reinforced walls in and around the shower and bath and in the toilet to serve as fixing points for grab rails (not required for masonry walls).

Adapted from Liveable Homes: liveablehomes.net.au

PERFORMANCE AND SUSTAINABILITY GUIDANCE

When planning a sustainable home, it's important to be clear about your objectives and use these to guide decisions during the design and build process. On a regulatory level, NatHERS is the only national scheme that needs be addressed (other than in NSW, which uses a state scheme called BASIX – see page 29). NatHERS is a performance-based rating system that describes the expected thermal performance of a home on a scale of 0–10. Simply put, the higher the star rating, the less energy is required to make it comfortable to live in. A score of 0 is akin to living outside; theoretically, a 10-star rated house shouldn't require any artificial heating or cooling to be comfortable year-round.

NatHERS scores are based on the simulated thermal performance of a building design, using specialist software by trained assessors. A number of factors will influence the result, including building orientation, building materials, insulation levels, windows and glazing type, and shading devices. Currently, the minimum performance rating required for new homes under the Building Code of Australia is six stars. All too often, NatHERS assessments are undertaken purely to demonstrate compliance with minimum standard requirements; however, it is also a useful tool to aid design by testing different design options. Proactive building designers and NatHERS assessors who are committed to a good design outcome will be open to this process.

The Nationwide House Energy Rating Scheme sets minimum energy-efficiency requirements for heating and cooling a home. The more stars, the less energy will be required to keep it thermally comfortable, and the more cost-effective it will be to run

For us, pursuing a 10-star NatHERS rating was about aiming high and testing a theory as much as anything, as in reality, a rating of 7.5 or above is considered a 'high-performance home' and can be expected to be comfortable for most of the year and be efficient to heat and cool. My bugbear was that air conditioning is often presented as an unavoidable item in a modern home when, in reality, in many parts of the country, and certainly in a mild climate like Perth, supplementary heating and cooling can largely be avoided if a house is designed, built and operated properly. Observing these principles makes a house cheaper to run and healthier to live in due to naturally stable internal temperatures.

One of the limitations of NatHERS is that it doesn't provide an indication of the overall energy efficiency of a home. Heating and cooling are typically responsible for the biggest energy demand (around 40%), so it's a good start, but things like water heating (around 25%), appliances and cooking (around 28%) and lighting (around 7%) aren't included.

It's also important to note that other resource efficiency factors that have significant environmental and carbon footprint implications, such as materials selection and water efficiency, are outside the scope of NatHERS. This is quite apart from issues such as indoor air quality and biodiversity. For this, you can look towards other sustainability frameworks for guidance, such as the HIA GreenSmart House Protocol. Although we looked at a variety of tools such as Green Star, One Planet Living and the Living Building Challenge, which were fascinating and a great source of ideas and information, we settled on GreenSmart as the most suitable framework for our project as it was created specifically for the Australian residential construction industry. See page 172 for the

GreenSmart objectives for our project and a summary of how we addressed the criteria for each protocol.

The Housing Industry of Australia (HIA) is a national industry association for Australian building professionals, and GreenSmart is the HIA's sustainability program. It aims to encourage a mainstream application of the benefits of environmentally responsible housing. The program provides training to participating builders and the certification of GreenSmart-accredited homes, which need to demonstrate a reduction in environmental impact across a range of areas including improved energy efficiency, reduced water usage, resource efficiency, reduced waste and improved energy management. The beauty of GreenSmart is that it is well-established in the industry, and provides a common language between a client and builder to shape the expectations of the build.

Achieving GreenSmart certification on a house requires evidence to be provided on how specific criteria relating to these protocol requirements have been achieved. We were guided by the protocols for the design and construction of both houses on the property, which were later accredited under the GreenSmart program. We found the protocol a useful way of ensuring our design intentions were achieved and specific initiatives were clearly understood and implemented by our builder.

BASIX

In New South Wales, an additional compliance assessment is required, known as the Building Sustainability Index, or BASIX. Like NatHERS, the BASIX assessment must be undertaken prior to a home being approved for construction. It was introduced by the NSW government in 2004 to improve the environmental performance of residential development, and requires a building design to meet minimum thermal performance requirements, as well as energy- and water-use reduction targets. These targets are reviewed and their stringency increased from time to time, with the goal of gradually improving the performance of homes. The BASIX assessment tool is capable of calculating the thermal performance of a dwelling; however, it is not as accurate or nuanced as the NatHERS software tools. For this reason, it is advisable to use a NatHERS energy rating to complete this part of the building performance assessment to ensure the best design outcome.

GREENSMART HOUSE PROTOCOL REQUIREMENTS

Energy Management: The ability of the householders to reduce operational energy consumption through passive solar design elements, appropriate construction methods for the climate, appropriate ventilation and the selection of energy-efficient fittings and appliances.

Water Management: The ability of the householders to reduce water consumption through the selection of water-efficient fittings and fixtures and the installation of alternative water supplies.

Material Selection: The selection and use of materials that can assist in reducing the environmental impact of the home during construction and as a finished home.

Indoor Air Quality Management: The selection and use of materials and building products that assist in creating a healthier home environment for occupants.

Universal Design: The layout and features of the home ensure that the current and future needs of the occupants, regardless of age or ability, can be met through simple adaptations.

Site Management: Ensuring construction work takes place in a way that minimises the removal of soil and sediment from the building site and prevents these from entering drains and nearby waterways.

Resource-Efficient Practice: Ensuring construction work is carried out in a way that minimises waste material generated, and ensuring appropriate storage during construction and removal from site at completion.

Adapted from HIA GreenSmart House Protocol Guideline, 2015

Northern Elevation

1. Evergreen native trees protect the eastern elevation of the house from hot morning sun.

2. Solar hot-water system.

3. Solar panels for energy generation.

4. Shared productive garden provides both houses with seasonal fresh food.

5. Deciduous trees provide shade in summer and allow sunlight in during winter.

6. Shade sails provide shade in summer and are taken down in winter to let sunlight in.

7. North-facing windows for winter solar gain.

CHAPTER 2

CLIMATE-RESPONSIVE DESIGN

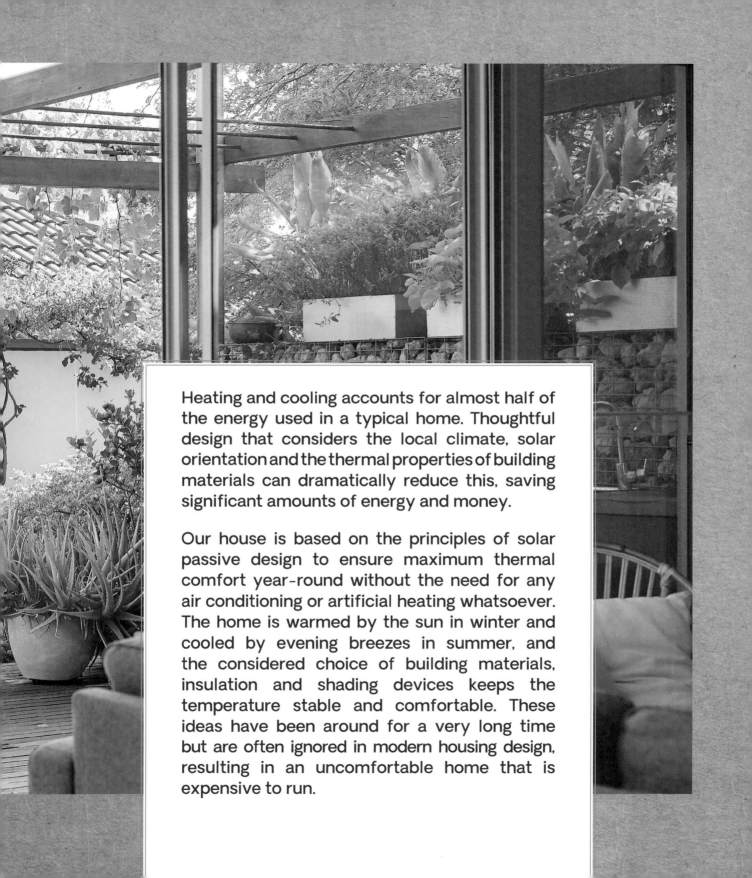

Heating and cooling accounts for almost half of the energy used in a typical home. Thoughtful design that considers the local climate, solar orientation and the thermal properties of building materials can dramatically reduce this, saving significant amounts of energy and money.

Our house is based on the principles of solar passive design to ensure maximum thermal comfort year-round without the need for any air conditioning or artificial heating whatsoever. The home is warmed by the sun in winter and cooled by evening breezes in summer, and the considered choice of building materials, insulation and shading devices keeps the temperature stable and comfortable. These ideas have been around for a very long time but are often ignored in modern housing design, resulting in an uncomfortable home that is expensive to run.

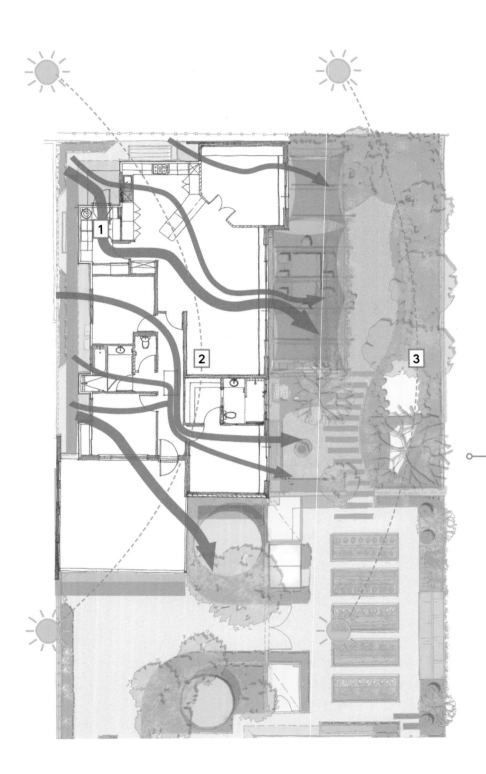

The building orientation, window placement and layout of Josh's house has been designed to capture warming winter sun and exclude hot summer sun, while cooling breezes flow through in summer.

1. Cooling breezes directed through the house in summer to purge heat and cool internal thermal mass.
2. Summer solar arc. Direct sunlight excluded from entering the house to reduce heat.
3. Winter solar arc. Sunlight captured to warm the house.

ORIENTATION, SOLAR GAIN AND SHADING

Correctly orientating a building to take advantage of warming winter sunshine (in cool/cold and temperate climate areas) and minimising unwanted hot summer sun (in all areas) is a fundamental first step in creating a comfortable and energy-efficient home.

The east–west orientation of our block of land meant that it was easy to orientate our building envelope the same way, exposing the north side of the building to maximum solar access. By designing the house to be long and narrow on the east–west axis, the eastern and western faces of the building are kept relatively small, which reduces exposure to hot morning and even hotter afternoon sun in summer.

By placing large windows on the northern side, low-angled winter sun streams into the house to warm it up in the winter. At its lowest point at the winter solstice (21 June), the sun is at an angle of 34.5 degrees at midday which is low enough to come in through windows and bathe the rooms of the entire northern side in sunshine. Zoning our living areas on this side of the house means that we make the most of the warmth and natural light.

At the spring and autumn equinoxes (21 September and 21 March), the sun is at 58 degrees at midday, which means less direct light penetrates the windows. On the summer solstice (21 December), the sun is high in the sky at 81.5 degrees at midday, meaning that little to no sun enters the windows. Even without any further shade management, this naturally occurring process of

having maximum solar penetration in winter, partial solar penetration in spring and autumn, and almost none in summer makes the home very comfortable.

The points at which the sun rises and sets also vary throughout the year, forming a narrow arc in winter and a much deeper arc in summer. At the spring and autumn equinoxes, it rises and sets due east and due west. This is important to understand to ensure that winter sun is not obscured, and summer sun is adequately screened out.

As a rule, the approach of designing to capture warming winter sun is appropriate for all cool/cold and temperate climate zones, including much of southern Australia; however, solar paths differ based on latitude, so it's important to design to the angles specific to your location. House comfort in all regions will benefit from minimising exposure to hot summer sun, but especially in hot and tropical climate zones, where protection from unwanted heat gain should be front of mind when orientating a building.

Correctly orientating a building to take advantage of warming winter sunshine and minimising unwanted hot summer sun is a fundamental first step in creating a comfortable and energy-efficient home

---

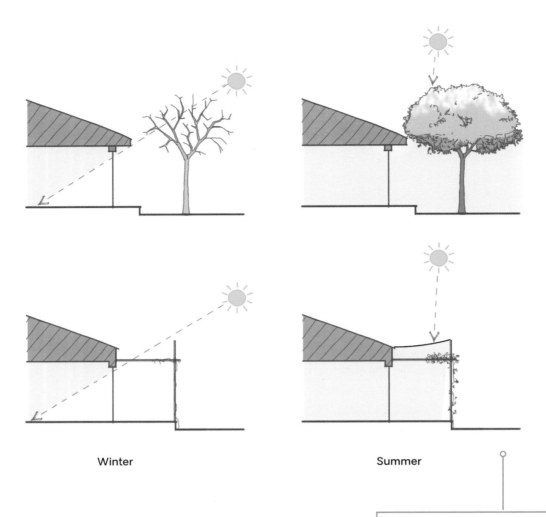

Winter   Summer

Additional shading can come in the form of trees, vines over trellis, awnings and shade sails. At our house, we have several shading strategies on the north side of the house. Firstly, shade sails were installed to provide a source of instant shade over the deck and northern face of the home. These are taken down in late autumn to allow winter sunlight into the home and put up again in late spring when we want shade again. A grapevine was planted on the pergola over the deck to provide additional summer shading and to soften the structure

ABOVE, SUN ANGLES: At Josh's house, devices such as eaves, shade sails and deciduous trees and vines are strategically used to provide shade to the northern side of the house in summer, while allowing sunshine through the windows in winter. Understanding the sun angles across the seasons is critical to making this work.

In the middle of winter, the north-facing living areas at Josh's house are bathed in sunlight, making them naturally warm and inviting.

DEALING WITH AWKWARD AND SMALL BLOCKS

Typically, east–west orientated blocks are ideal for climate responsive design in cool/cold and temperate climate zones where winter solar gain is desirable; however, on small, narrow blocks in built-up areas, overshadowing from neighbouring buildings is likely to be an issue. In this instance, north–south blocks are preferred as they allow for north-facing living areas to receive winter sun, and adjacent buildings can provide shade from summer morning and afternoon sun. On deep blocks, internal courtyards can be used to allow winter sun into other parts of the building.

The graphic opposite illustrates different ways that houses can be positioned to capture sunshine, including blocks on awkward angles, outside of due east–west or due north–south. In all scenarios, living areas should be zoned to the north to receive maximum value from northern sunlight. In areas of double-storey homes, where overshadowing from neighbours is a problem, consider zoning the living areas on the upper floor to be clear of obstructions. A deviation of 15 to 20 degrees off north–south, and 20 to 30 degrees off east–west can be managed, with the greater deviation favouring winter solar gain.

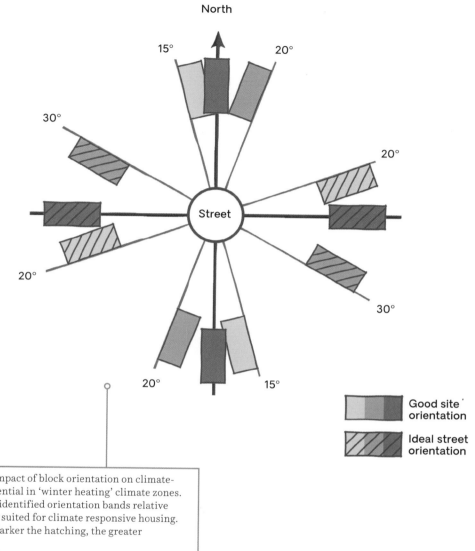

North

15°   20°

30°

20°   20°

20°

30°

20°   15°

Street

Good site orientation

Ideal street orientation

BLOCK ORIENTATION: Impact of block orientation on climate-responsive design potential in 'winter heating' climate zones. The blocks within the identified orientation bands relative to the street are better suited for climate responsive housing. On this diagram, the darker the hatching, the greater the suitability.
(Illustration adapted from YourHome: yourhome.gov.au)

visually. Being deciduous, it naturally loses its leaves in winter and lets sunlight through. We have also included several deciduous trees (see Chapter 7) to provide shade over the broader area, including over paths and parts of the garden, to create a pleasant microclimate.

Even structures such as the western boundary fence and rainwater tank have been put to use, protecting the eastern and western sides of the house against hot morning and afternoon sun.

The northern elevation of Josh's house during winter,
shortly after construction.

The northern elevation of Josh's house during summer, six years on.

Generous window openings have been positioned to capture prevailing breezes, ensuring good cross ventilation.

CROSS VENTILATION

Just as warming winter sun can be used to naturally heat a home, cross ventilation can be used to purge unwanted heat in summer and cool a home down. A well-ventilated house is also healthier to be in because carbon dioxide and other gases exhaled by humans and pets, plus all the other smells and particles that are part of life, are flushed out regularly.

The narrow nature of our house design also makes for better cross ventilation. By only being two rooms deep, air easily moves through the building. Our prevailing cooling summer breezes come from the south-west, and we have carefully located windows and doors to allow unobstructed pathways for air to pass through all the rooms without getting trapped. The window openings are larger on the leeward side than they are on the windward side. While this might seem counterintuitive, it greatly improves cross ventilation as this arrangement creates a zone of negative pressure inside the house, pulling air through the home even on relatively still nights.

Cross ventilation can be used to purge unwanted heat in summer and cool a home down

---

Window type is important. We've chosen sliding windows and louvres on the south (windward) side of the home, rather than awning types, as they allow more air through. Louvres (which typically have their panels oriented to bridge the shortest span) are best suited to situations where window aperture size is constrained and good airflow is required, as they allow maximum airflow through when open compared to other window types. Good-quality products that create a decent seal when closed are relatively expensive so should be prioritised where they will have the greatest impact. On the northern (leeward) side, we have sliding doors, as well as sashless vertical sliding windows to maximise the openings. By installing security screens over the windows we feel comfortable leaving the windows open at night, including when we go out, and they provide the dual function of insect screens. We've also installed magnetic catches on all the doors to stop them slamming if caught by the breeze.

CONSIDERATIONS FOR HOT AND TROPICAL CLIMATES

In hot humid (tropical) climates and hot dry climates with no winter heating requirements, direct sunlight and radiant heat from nearby structures should be excluded year-round by using large overhanging eaves, verandas and trees to shade the external walls, openings and glazing, while maximising exposure to prevailing cooling breezes.

In areas north of the Tropic of Capricorn, where the sun passes overhead in the southern part of the sky during summer, both the northern and southern sides of the house require shading. To prevent low morning and afternoon sun from heating up the house, the size of east- and west-facing wall areas should be minimised and windows in these walls should be avoided unless well shaded. External shading on all sides of the house, particularly of glazing, will reduce unwanted heat gain during the day. Minimising hard surfaces and heavy materials around the home will also help with keeping cool by reducing thermal mass.

Cooling through natural ventilation requires good exposure of the building and its windows to the dominant breezes.

In tropical areas, natural ventilation for passive cooling is usually best achieved by having long, narrow buildings orientated towards prevailing cooling breezes, with windows on opposite or adjacent walls in each room to enable cooling winds to easily pass through. Louvres can be particularly effective here. Large eaves and verandas are also useful for excluding rain entry through open windows during heavy rain events.

In hot dry areas, airflow from outside during the day may be undesirable as it can increase heat gain and remove moisture from our bodies. At such times, it is best to exclude external airflow unless it is moistened and cooled. It is often best to close the home during the day and open the house at night to flush out stored heat.

The concrete slab and internal brick walls at Josh's house provide thermal mass that helps to stabilise internal temperature.

CONSTRUCTION MATERIALS: LIGHTWEIGHT VERSUS HEAVY MASS

While building materials with high thermal mass contribute significantly to thermal stability in a home, lightweight construction materials such as timber, structural insulated panels (SIPS) and lightweight cladding can have benefits in a build also. Lightweight materials are easier to transport (so may be favourable for remote sites) and they are typically more flexible and cost-effective to work with on sloping sites, and where slab-on-ground construction is not suitable due to soil type or environmental sensitivity. Lightweight materials will often have a lower embodied energy value than manufactured high–thermal mass materials such as concrete and bricks, meaning less energy is consumed (and carbon emitted) through their manufacture and transport; however, this is dependent on how the materials are produced and how they are transported.

Lightweight materials are the preferred option for hot and tropical climates as they will retain less heat. In cool and temperate climates, homes built from lightweight materials are likely to require more active heating and cooling and attention to insulation and draught sealing becomes more critical (see Chapter 8).

THERMAL MASS

Thermal mass is a term used to describe the ability of a material to absorb and store heat energy. Heavy materials such as brick, stone and concrete have high thermal mass, while lightweight materials such as timber and plasterboard have low thermal mass. These characteristics can be used to advantage to improve the thermal properties of a home. For example, high–thermal mass materials take longer to heat up and take longer to cool down than lighter-weight materials, and are ideally used inside the house to help stabilise internal temperature. Concrete floors and internal brick walls are good examples of high–thermal mass building materials. On the other hand, lightweight materials such as timber cladding quickly lose their heat; hence, they are useful when this is desirable.

Thermal mass is the ability of a material to absorb and store heat energy and it can be used to advantage to improve the thermal properties of a home

In our home, the sun that penetrates through the northern windows in winter hits the concrete slab floor and warms it up over the course of the day. At night, the heat is slowly released, keeping the house warm. Some of the heat is also transferred into the internal brick walls, which are insulated from the outside, to be stored through the day and then radiated out in the evening, contributing to a comfortable temperature.

Internal thermal mass can also be put to work in summer. The cool night-time breezes that move through the home not only remove stale, warm air, they also cool down the temperature of the concrete and bricks, making the temperature comfortable for the following day.

High–thermal mass materials should be protected from unwanted and uncontrolled heat gain or heat loss. Having hot summer sun hitting a concrete slab floor, for example, will quickly make a room uncomfortably hot. Likewise, a masonry wall will transfer heat from the inside of a building to the outside in winter if it is not properly insulated. In situations where mass can't be protected, the use of lightweight well-insulated materials that don't readily retain or transfer heat is usually preferred.

INSULATION

Insulation reduces the movement of heat in and out of a house, helping to keep it warmer in winter and cooler in summer. The inclusion of insulation in a building is one of the more cost-effective ways to make a home thermally comfortable, but it's important to understand how it works and the impact it makes on the home's performance in relation to the rest of the building fabric (floor, walls, windows and roof). Understanding the function of insulation will help you to select the right type to complement the design features and construction type of your home.

There are two main types of insulation: reflective insulation, which is used to reduce the penetration of radiant heat, and bulk insulation, which slows the movement of conductive and convective heat. The performance of insulation is referred to as R-value (thermal resistance value). The higher the R-value, the more effective the material is at preventing heat transfer, with most common housing insulation material values ranging from 0.01 to 7, depending on their type and intended application.

Insulation reduces the movement of heat in and out of a house, helping to keep it warmer in winter and cooler in summer. It is one of the more cost-effective ways to make a home thermally comfortable

---

Bulk insulation works by trapping air within insulating material and includes products such as batts, wool blankets and blown cellulose fibre. Reflective insulation uses a reflective surface to block radiant heat. There are also composite products available which combine the properties of both bulk and reflective insulation.

Modern bulk insulation such as glasswool and rockwool batts don't settle in the way some of the older-style paper and wool products used to, and the fibres don't degrade. However, it's important to make sure that once laid, it is not disturbed. If it is moved out of the way, it needs to be reinstated.

The Building Code of Australia requires minimum R-values to be met for walls and roofs/ceilings as an energy efficiency measure. These vary according to climate zone. The R-values are based on combined values for a particular 'construction system'. For example, a wall may contain multiple layers of building material, such as external cladding, waterproof membrane, timber frame, reflective foil, bulk insulation batts and plasterboard, as well as the nominated air gaps specified in the wall design as required for preventing moisture issues. The minimum R-value requirements are based on the insulating performance of the wall as a whole. If insulation is installed under roof sheeting and in the ceiling, then the combined R-values can be used to meet (or exceed) BCA requirements.

High–thermal mass walls that have a density of over 200 kg per square metre have reduced minimum R-value requirements in the BCA on the basis of their thermal inertia, that is, they take a long time to heat up and cool down. Ideally, all walls – regardless of mass – should have an insulating layer to separate them from

SOLAR PASSIVE OR PASSIVE HOUSE?

The terms 'solar passive' and 'passive house' are often confused and used interchangeably, but they are different approaches to energy-efficient building, although not mutually exclusive. Solar passive utilises climate-responsive design to naturally warm and cool a building and is based on the principles of optimising building orientation, using thermal mass effectively and insulating to create a comfortable and stable internal temperature for occupation. Passive House (or Passivhaus) also aims to create thermally comfortable, low-energy buildings, but with an emphasis on creating a highly insulated and sealed building envelope, and the use of very efficient mechanical ventilation to condition the internal spaces and regulate internal air quality. The Passive House approach is very compelling when lightweight construction materials are used, or when adequate solar gain is limited due to block orientation or excessive shading from neighbouring structures.

For more information visit:
passivehouseaustralia.org

the external environment to minimise uncontrolled heat loss or heat gain, in conjunction with shading devices. This also applies to on-ground concrete slabs in cool/cold and hot climate zones, where heat can transfer in and out of a building to the earth below, or to the atmosphere where the sides are exposed to the sun and ambient external temperatures.

It's important to note that more insulation isn't always best. For example, an over-insulated house that heats up through excessive solar penetration and has poor natural ventilation will become a hot box. Thermal modelling using NatHERS-accredited software is the best way to determine the extent of insulation required, where climate zone, building design and construction type are all taken into consideration. This will ensure maximum comfort levels are achieved without over-specifying.

At our house, we installed a R1.25 50 mm composite reflective foil and bulk insulation under the roof sheeting to stabilise the temperature of the roof cavity and prevent condensation, and R4 glass fibre bulk insulation batts in the ceiling. In the walls, we used a combination of an R0.015 composite reflective foil and foam-cell insulation in the cavity brick walls, and this same product along with R2.5 glass fibre bulk insulation batts in our timber frame and reverse brick veneer walls (see Chapter 3). In our climate zone, and with our building design and construction type, this is what was required to achieve a 10-star NatHERS rating and to have a home that is comfortable year-round without additional heating or cooling.

It's important to note that more insulation isn't always best – an over-insulated house that heats up through excessive solar penetration and has poor natural ventilation will become a hot box

ABOVE: Bulk and reflective foam-cell insulation being installed during construction of the timber-framed walls.
BOTTOM LEFT: Reflective foam-cell insulation is installed in the cavity in between the 'leaves' of the double-brick walls.
BOTTOM RIGHT: Glass fibre bulk insulation is highly effective at trapping air and is also very durable.

CHAPTER 3

BUILDING FABRIC & MATERIALS

The choice of building materials has a big impact on the sustainability of a home. The amount of energy required to manufacture, transport and maintain materials is an important consideration, as is the impact of where the materials were sourced from, as well as what happens to them at the end of a building's life. Material choice will also influence the thermal performance of a home, that is, the amount of energy required to keep a home at a comfortable temperature.

With our build we intentionally selected materials that are commonly used by the local building industry to keep costs down, and to demonstrate that high-performance houses can be built using standard materials and by using regular trades. There are a range of alternative construction materials available that may have better environmental credentials than what we built with but, invariably, they come at a cost and may limit your choice in builders. But don't let that deter you from being ambitious with the use of 'traditional' alternative materials, such as stone, rammed earth or straw bale, or more contemporary materials such as SIPS (structural insulated panels) or hempcrete, if that's what you want to do – this is a field that is constantly changing and some things that were exotic when we built may be more practical today. However, it's important to consider the materials in a house as a series of components that work together to make the home comfortable. The following sections describe these components that collectively make up the 'building fabric' of a house, including floor, walls, roof and windows, and show how the characteristics of particular materials influence performance.

ABOVE: In Perth's mild climate, the 100 mm thick ground-coupled slab at Josh's house helps to keep the internal temperature stable.

LEFT: The concrete slab was painted as a decorative finish, rather than covered in timber or carpet, to keep the thermal mass exposed.

SLAB

Most new houses are built using slab-on-ground construction that combines the floor and footing in a common concrete structure. The size and depth of the footings will be determined by the engineering requirements of the building and site conditions. The depth of the slab typically ranges between 75 mm and 100 mm and includes a steel reinforcement mesh. We chose to install a 100 mm deep slab for additional thermal mass.

Concrete slabs are a good source of thermal mass to stabilise internal temperature. In mild climates such as in Perth, Sydney and Brisbane, the direct coupling of a slab to the ground has the added benefit of utilising the stable temperature of the ground. In cold climates, or if underfloor heating is used, then slab insulation is required, both under the slab and around the edges, to prevent heat loss. In hot climates, insulating the edges of the slab with expanded foam is good practice to prevent heating up of the slab from adjacent ground that is exposed to the sun.

SLAB CONSIDERATIONS FOR OTHER CLIMATES

Direct slab-on-ground construction is well suited to mild climate regions like coastal NSW, Perth and Brisbane, where the connection of the slab to the ground keeps it warmer in winter and cooler in summer than the ambient air, thus assisting with the comfort of the house.

In cool and cold regions, slab insulation is important to prevent heat loss from inside the building into the ground. 'Waffle pod' slabs, which incorporate polystyrene slabs in between a narrow internal concrete beam and a perimeter edge beam, can be used for this. Waffle pod slabs provide a range of benefits in addition to insulation from the ground, including reduced concrete use. Edge insulation should also be installed and is also useful in hot climates to prevent the conduction of surface heat into a building.

If in-slab heating and/or cooling systems are being used (see Chapter 4), then whole-slab insulation such as polystyrene sheeting should be installed to reduce unwanted heat transfer in and out of the slab.

CONSIDERATIONS FOR
HIGH FIRE DANGER ZONES

Bushfire is a real and ever-present risk in Australia. Growing concern over community safety has resulted in the introduction of building compliance requirements under the National Construction Code (NCC) and associated standards to improve the resistance of buildings to fire attack in bushfire-prone areas.

Fire protection compliance measures for houses (and structures such as sheds, outbuildings and decks) vary according to the level of risk and likely severity of bushfire attack. Sites are classified by Bushfire Attack Level, or BAL, according to the following scale:

- BAL-Low: Very low risk (bushfire resistant construction not required)

- BAL-12.5: Low risk

- BAL-19: Moderate risk

- BAL-29: High risk

- BAL-40: Very high risk

- BAL-FZ: Extreme risk (Flame Zone)

BAL ratings can be assigned to urban areas as well as rural, and are influenced by factors such as proximity to forest or bushland, the makeup and density of the vegetation, and slope and environmental conditions. Classification of BAL-rated areas are under the jurisdiction of states and territories and may alter subject to review and changing circumstances.

BAL rating compliance must be demonstrated in building design documentation and accompanied by a BAL assessment report and certificate prepared by an accredited assessor. This is typically reviewed by local government at the planning approval and building licence stage.

Determining whether a BAL rating applies to a site of interest is an important consideration when choosing where to build as there may be construction cost implications ranging from relatively minor in low-risk areas to significant in high- and extreme-risk areas. Choice of building materials and design outcomes may also be impacted.

Early consideration of BAL requirements in the design process can help to keep construction costs down, rather than having to implement expensive add-on measures to meet compliance. There may also be cost-effective opportunities to achieve both improved building thermal performance and BAL compliance outcomes through choice of building fabric and construction methods that result in a well-sealed building envelope.

WALLS

Walls do more than just hold the roof up. They play a critical role in the thermal performance of a home. In our build, we used a combination of wall types to maximise the best properties of each. Our original concept design included rammed recycled rubble walls for the main internal walls to provide thermal mass while also reusing a waste material. We soon discovered that the cost was beyond our budget.

The first external wall type is reverse brick veneer. Standard brick veneer walls are commonly used around Australia. These have a single leaf of brickwork on the outside face. Plasterboard on timber or light steel framing is used on the inside, with insulation in the frame. With reverse brick veneer, the brickwork is located on the inside face to provide additional thermal mass inside the home. The outside is clad with a weatherproof cladding – weatherboards – and the cavity is filled with insulation (bulk and reflective foil) to isolate the internal brick mass from the outside environment. Importantly, the internal brick wall is coated with wet plaster rather than plasterboard, as this results in better direct contact between the inside air and the wall mass.

In Perth, reverse brick veneer is more expensive than either double brick or timber-framed walls. We limited the use of this construction type to the eastern and western sides of the house where we would be able to make the most of its performance properties. The eastern and western sides of the house get maximum exposure to hot morning and afternoon sun in summer. The use of weatherboards, which are low in density

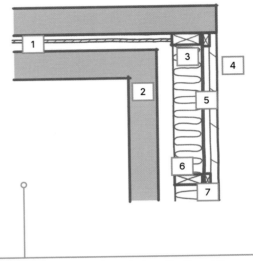

Reverse brick veneer walls have the benefit of providing internal thermal mass, combined with good insulation in the wall framing.

1. Reflective foam-cell insulation
2. Brick
3. Bulk insulation
4. Weatherboards over moisture membrane
5. Reflective foam-cell insulation
6. Timber wall stud
7. Timber batten

compared to brick, is a sensible choice as they absorb less heat. We also like the look of them and they suit the character of the other houses in our street. We chose a cement fibre product (as opposed to the traditional wood type) because they require a lot less maintenance.

The second external wall type used in our house is double-brick cavity wall with reflective closed-cell insulation. In Perth, this is the most common and cost-effective wall construction method. The downside is that they absorb a lot of heat when exposed to hot sun. They also have a high embodied energy value compared to other walling systems such as timber

ABOVE LEFT: Timber frame panels form part of the walling system.
ABOVE RIGHT: Weatherboards being installed as the external cladding over moisture membrane.
BELOW: Bricks being laid to form the inside layer of the reverse brick veneer walling system.

frame. For this reason, we limited the use of double-brick walls to where we needed high thermal mass and where the external faces could be adequately shielded from direct summer sun.

The third external wall type is timber frame, with weatherboard external cladding and plasterboard internal cladding, with bulk and reflective insulation in between. This walling method has the lowest embodied energy value of the three systems we used due to the use of plantation pine timber and the absence of brick. The timber-framed wall type was used for the southern wall of the house where adequate mass was already present in the concrete slab and internal brick walls.

Internal walls in our house are generally plastered single-leaf brickwork with some double-brick walls used to add additional thermal mass to the main living areas, as well as to provide sound insulation to selected rooms.

Completed walls on the eastern side of the front house. The double-brick wall is shaded from the sun by a large veranda awning. The wall in the foreground is a reverse brick veneer wall. The insulation between the external weatherboard layer and internal brick layer helps to keep the room (and house) cool.

ABOVE LEFT: Timber-framed roof.
ABOVE RIGHT: Steel roof sheeting.
BOTTOM LEFT: Light-coloured roof materials reflect light and reduce heat build-up.
BOTTOM RIGHT: An insulation blanket sits under the roof sheeting to reduce condensation and heat transfer.

ROOF

The roof framing is a conventional gable timber construction which suits the style of the house and vernacular of the neighbourhood. We chose steel cladding rather than tiles because of the availability of light-coloured products, which reduce heat absorbance. The relative light weight of steel sheeting compared to tiles also means that it retains less heat. Also, my experience has been that working on a roof covered in steel sheeting is much easier than on a tiled one. We selected a corrugated roof sheet profile because, once again, it suited the style of our house. There are more contemporary profiles available to suit more modern house designs.

> We chose steel cladding rather than tiles because of the availability of light-coloured products, which reduce heat absorbance

The rectangular design of the house made for a simple gabled roof design, which makes for easy installation and reduced wastage of materials that can result from complicated roof designs. The combination of the light-coloured and light-weight roof sheeting, plus the insulation blanket installed beneath it to reduce heat transfer and condensation, has resulted in a steady temperature in the roof cavity, making it well suited to be used as a storage space. Increased roof cavity ventilation is provided by a small roof-mounted extraction fan unit. The vent is self-powering via a small solar photovoltaic (PV) panel attached to the vent shroud and only comes on when the temperature exceeds 28°C.

IMPACT OF ROOF COLOUR ON HOUSE TEMPERATURE

The colour of roofs attracts lots of commentary, with black roofs often criticised as being a poor choice due to concerns over heat generation in summer and the impact that this is likely to have on energy use for cooling. Dark-coloured materials absorb more solar radiation than light-coloured materials, which generates heat. Research has shown that if a building is properly insulated, the additional heat from a dark-coloured roof, regardless of the material, is unlikely to have a significant impact on the internal temperature; however, if roof and ceiling insulation is inadequate, or poorly installed, then heat is likely to penetrate the building. But on a wider scale, the concentration of dark-coloured roofs in a particular area, as is often seen in new housing estates, will contribute to the build-up of localised urban heat, impacting human comfort and increasing water use for surrounding vegetation. This is less likely to occur with light-toned roofs that reflect solar radiation and lightweight roofing materials that lose heat quickly.

Additional rafters were installed in the roof structure and boards laid to create a storage area with access via a pull-down ladder in the hallway. The ladder also makes it easy to get into the roof space to access wiring and water supply pipework if needed, plus inspect for rodents and other pests.

TOP: This graph shows how the building materials work as a system to keep the house comfortable. The roof surface gets hot during the day, but quickly cools. The roof insulation blanket helps to keep the roof cavity cooler than outside, despite the hot roof surface. Hot air gets trapped at the ceiling until it is flushed out. The slab and internal brick walls remain a relatively consistent temperature due their high thermal mass.
BOTTOM: This graph compares the temperature inside the living room with the outside temperature across the year at midday. Internal temperatures remain steady and comfortable, despite wide variation of external temperatures.

Vertical Profile Temperatures

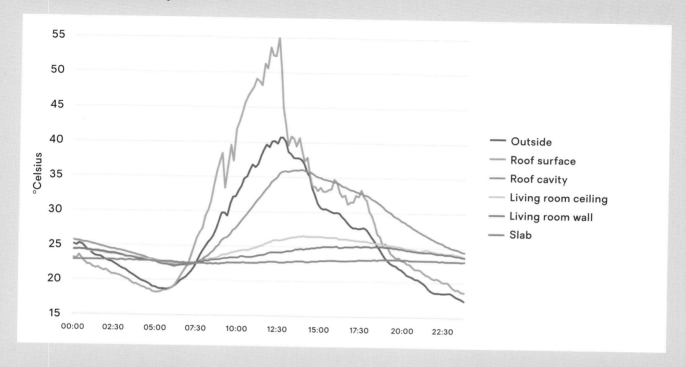

Annual Temperature Profile

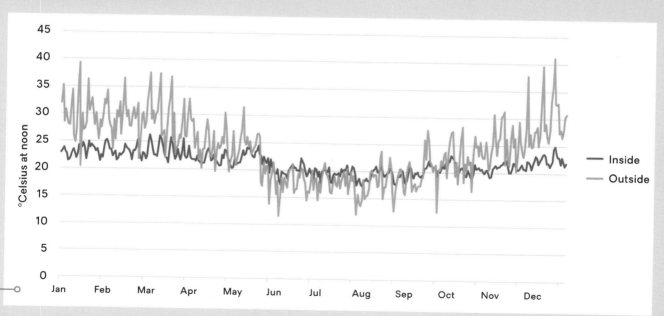

WINDOWS AND WINDOW TREATMENTS

Window location and type of glazing play a key role in the thermal performance of a home, with over a third of heating and cooling energy typically lost via windows. If positioned thoughtfully, windows can be used to warm a house in winter and help keep it cool in summer, whereas poorly thought-out window placement, size and glass selection will result in unwanted heat entry in summer and significant heat loss in winter.

The solar passive design of our home includes carefully considered window positioning and seasonal protection. The glazing chosen for the windows, as well as window treatments, such as curtains, blinds and shutters are also important. It's the combination of hard-working features together with good passive design that keeps the hot summer sun off the glass.

We used single pane low-e (low emissivity) glass on all windows except one, where double glazing was used. Low-e glass has a laminated internal layer which allows light to pass through, but reduces heat loss. It is more expensive than standard glazing, but it performs much better.

Heat loss in winter is further reduced through the inclusion of curtains that hang from ceiling to floor, which have been installed on all the large north-facing windows. This traps air and effectively acts as insulation. The ceiling includes a hidden pelmet, which screens the

In addition to helping to heat the home, the large north-facing windows in Josh's house ensure good natural ventilation and connect inside and outside living spaces.

curtain track, and also helps to trap air, further adding to the insulating effect.

The curtains were made using a blockout-weight curtain lining. The blockout is achieved by coating a cotton, or polyester/cotton, basic base cloth with three layers of acrylic foam (two layers of off-white and a layer of black in between) to control the light. Acrylic was chosen as it has the highest resistance to UV. The coating is mechanically spread onto the fabric, smoothed, heat set and then treated with a stain-resistant finish.

In the winter months, the curtains are opened so that sunlight passes through the north-facing windows

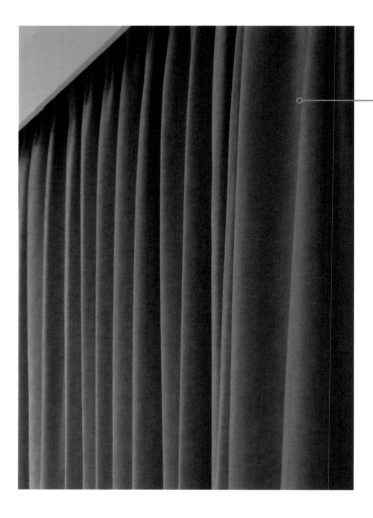

Curtains are an effective way to prevent heat loss through windows. At Josh's house, double-layered curtains have been used, which trap air in between and act as insulation. The top of the curtains sit behind a pelmet which hides the rail and also helps to trap air, increasing the insulation performance.

during the day to warm up the concrete floor and internal brick walls (thermal mass). At dusk, the curtains are closed to trap this internal heat to keep the living areas thermally comfortable. In the summer, the orientation of the building combined with window placement means that direct sunlight entry into the home is minimal; however, there are periods during late spring and early autumn where some sun does enter, and this is where curtains (and blinds) assist to help block out unwanted heat gain. The curtains also assist with acoustics by absorbing sound.

The double-glazed window sits above the sink in the kitchen, on the southern side of our open-plan living area, and is a slider to assist with internal cross ventilation. Double glazing consists of two panels of glass set in the one sealed frame, with inert gas in between (typically argon). Double glazing dramatically reduces heat flow and while it is very effective, it is also expensive. The inclusion of curtains above the kitchen sink wasn't practical, which is why we opted for double glazing in this location as the most effective solution for minimising heat loss.

> Aluminium-coated blinds were chosen for the large sliding glass doors on the northern side of the living area because of their high solar reflectance

Blinds and shutters were also included to assist with light control, glare management and privacy throughout the house. Aluminium-coated blinds were chosen for the large sliding glass doors on the northern side of the living area because of their high solar reflectance. They provide good glare control, as well as 'view through' characteristics. Heat transfer is also minimised as the metallisation reduces transmission of solar radiation. Timber shutters with adjustable horizontal louvres were chosen for the southern rooms as they can be tilted in such a way as to reduce light entry while still allowing breezes to pass through – two very important functions when balancing effective cross ventilation with sleeping children.

GLAZING FOR OTHER CLIMATES

In cool and cold climates, double glazing is the new standard in an energy-efficient home, and as it becomes more common, costs are coming down. Double glazing reduces thermal conductivity by around 50%, and the wider the gap between the panes, the better the insulation value. Choosing windows with timber or PVC (polyvinyl chloride) frames will also improve performance as these materials are poor thermal conductors when compared to aluminium (which is commonly used) so will transfer less heat.

Glazing can vary in its ability to allow solar radiation into a building and this is described as the solar heat gain coefficient or SHGC. The greater the SHGC, the greater the degree of solar radiation penetration. In cool, cold and temperate climates, where winter solar gain is desirable, high SHGC is best, but the windows should be well protected from summer sun to reduce heat entry. In hot and tropical areas, low-SHGC glazing is more appropriate, in conjunction with adequate window shading.

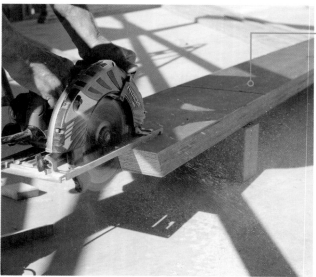

LEFT: LOSP-treated pine was used for structural timbers at Josh's house as it is considered a safer option than other products such as CCA treatment.

RIGHT: Rather than using a chemical treatment for termite control, a physical barrier was created using fine stainless-steel mesh. The highly durable material is laid across points where termites typically enter a building, such as around the perimeter walls, and where services such as plumbing and electrical conduits penetrate the slab.

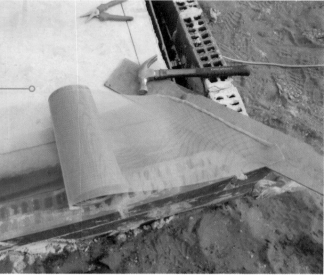

TERMITE CONTROL

Effective termite control is important to protect the longevity of your home and it is also a requirement under the Building Code of Australia, meaning that your builder will need to address it properly. Chemical protection is the cheapest and most common; however, there have been significant advances in low-toxicity methods with reduced environmental impact.

Effective termite control is important to protect the longevity of your home

The termite mesh is secured in place and the location marked for easy inspection.

In our build, in addition to preferencing timber treated with a lower toxicity treatment using light organic solvent preservative (LOSP) rather than copper chrome arsenate (CCA) for our wall and roof framing, we opted for a physical barrier for termite exclusion. This involved the installation of stainless-steel mesh around the perimeter of the building at the interface between the slab and walls, as well as around all slab penetrations such as plumbing and electrical pipes and conduits. The mesh prevents termites moving from under the ground into the building.

This approach is more expensive than chemical barrier methods but has the advantage of not requiring ongoing applications and eliminates the use of potentially harmful substances. Importantly, the external ground level must always be kept below the mesh barrier so the perimeter of the building can be readily inspected over time for termite bridging. This is good practice in any case as it avoids situations where moisture can move from garden soil mounded against a wall into a building, where it can damage building materials and potentially lead to compromised indoor air quality.

It's important that external soil levels, including surface treatments such as gravel or mulch, are kept beneath the termite mesh. This makes it easy to see during inspections if termites have bridged the physical barrier.

INDOOR AIR QUALITY

There's a growing body of evidence linking some health problems to poor indoor air quality. These range from mild symptoms such as headaches, tiredness or lethargy, to more severe effects such as aggravation of asthma and allergies. Some everyday household chemicals may have worse effects over the longer term. Common pollutants (and their sources) to be aware of include:

- Nitrogen dioxide from gas combustion.

- Carbon monoxide from fuel combustion resulting from cars idling in enclosed garages.

- Formaldehyde found in pressed-wood products and glues in consumer products.

- Volatile organic compounds (VOCs) in cleaning products and new building products such as paints, sealants and carpets.

- Mould spores from damp rooms and bathrooms.

- Carbon dioxide from people breathing and the burning of fuels in poorly ventilated rooms.

Good indoor air quality can be achieved through sensible design and product choices.

Key Considerations

Use Natural Ventilation: As new homes are becoming increasingly well sealed, we need to ensure they are well ventilated. Encourage breezes and convection currents to draw fresh air in. If windows are closed for security or noise reasons, install vents to ensure adequate ventilation.

Minimise Moisture: Avoid mould growth by lessening moisture levels. In brick homes, fit a damp-proof course to prevent moisture migrating from the ground into the wall, referred to as rising damp, and make sure outside soil levels are kept beneath this. Locate bathrooms on the northern side of the house to increase exposure to sunlight; make sure they have operable windows to allow in fresh air and are fitted with a suitably sized extraction fan. Likewise, a kitchen extraction fan should be sized and installed in line with relevant standards.

Ensure Building Security Allows Ventilation: Install security products, such as steel window screens or a zoned alarm, that make you feel secure but also allow you to regulate airflow.

Consider Mechanical Ventilation: Standard ducted air conditioning systems recirculate indoor air but do not introduce fresh air from outdoors. Consider installing mechanical ventilation systems to improve ventilation of fresh air into your home if natural cross ventilation is not possible or practical because of climate. Evaporative cooling systems are often used in hot, low-humidity areas because they are cheap to run; however, they increase indoor humidity and may increase levels of mould. If one is installed, make sure the system is sized, operated and maintained correctly to reduce the risk of this occurring.

Minimise Carpet: If new carpets are fixed with adhesives, these may contain VOCs. Underlay can also be a source. If possible, use low-emission products. Unroll the carpet in a well-ventilated area and air it for several days before it is installed.

Consider Other Sources of VOCs: Before specifying products such as tiled, vinyl, linoleum or polished floors, check whether there are likely to be any VOCs present, either in the product itself or in other products used to lay it (e.g. adhesives) or to seal the floor covering (e.g. varnishes and paints) and for maintenance products such as cleaning fluids and polishes. Ask suppliers whether there are low-VOC alternatives. The same applies for curtains and furnishings.

Wood-burning Heaters: Poorly installed or badly maintained wood-burning heaters can be a major source of fine combustion particles and gases. Ensure the flue or vent is properly designed and installed and is regularly maintained. Burn only well-seasoned wood.

Gas Appliances: If you decide to use gas, then vent gas appliances to the outside. If the use of unvented heaters is unavoidable, buy only low-NOx (nitrous oxide) appliances, and don't operate them in confined spaces for long periods of time. Ventilate the heated area with fixed wall vents (compulsory in some states).

Seal Doors Between Garage and Home: Exhaust from petrol and diesel engines contains many pollutants. Design a garage to stand apart from your home if possible. If attached, make sure the adjoining door is well fitted and securely sealed against leaks.

Adapted from Your Home: yourhome.gov.au

CHAPTER 4

ELECTRICAL FIT-OUT

Reducing household energy use starts with good building design. A well-designed house needs less mechanical heating and cooling to remain comfortable and will be naturally lit to reduce the need for daytime artificial lighting. Appliance selection is also important, especially for heating and cooling, which accounts for around 40% of typical household energy use, and hot water heating, which accounts for a further 20%.

The expansion of government standards in industry combined with rising energy costs has driven significant improvements in the efficiency of household appliances, and has helped make technologies such as highly efficient LED lights mainstream. Likewise, appliances that were once considered high-end, such as heat pump hot-water systems and induction cooktops, are now becoming the norm. The fully electric house is now a reality. Electric cars are the next step as we transition to a future where our homes and our vehicles can run completely on renewable energy. Considerations for solar energy generation and storage, and how we have applied these at our house, are covered in Chapter 5.

HOT WATER HEATING

When designing our home back in 2012, the prevailing wisdom for choosing a low energy–low carbon hot water solution was to use a solar thermal hot-water system with an instantaneous gas booster unit. These systems work by collecting the sun's heat via a solar thermal collector bed and transferring it into water. The hot water can be stored in a tank mounted on the roof next to the collector, or on the ground. The booster kicks in to provide additional heating when the sun's energy is not adequate (e.g. during cloudy weather in winter) or if the stored hot water is used up before more water can be naturally heated.

The use of an instantaneous gas booster was favoured over an electric booster because it produces less carbon when burned compared to grid electricity, which is typically generated by a combination of coal and gas (depending on the local generation mix). The energy conversion is also more efficient because of the energy loss in transmitting electricity long distances from where it is generated to where it is used.

This thinking informed the selection of our first hot-water unit. We chose a system that allowed for the solar thermal collector and storage tank to be mounted on the roof (see image on page 83), along with the instantaneous gas booster. Combining these components minimised heat losses between collector and storage tank, and between the tank and booster. We located the unit on the roof equidistant to the locations where hot water is used (bathroom, en suite, kitchen and laundry) to avoid lengthy runs between hot-water service and end uses, which means lower

Air source heat pump hot-water systems operate using similar principles as reverse cycle air conditioning and are highly efficient.

heat losses and less wasted water while waiting for the water to warm up. Generally, we were pretty happy with the system, but were surprised by how much boosting was required, even when the thermostat was set to the minimum required (60°C for a storage system).

The continuing decrease in cost of domestic solar photovoltaic (PV) systems has shifted the landscape so that heating water using electricity produced from solar PV has become increasingly practical, especially when combined with highly efficient systems like heat pumps, which have also come down in price. Heat pumps work on a similar principle to reverse cycle air conditioners. They draw heat from the air using a closed cycle refrigerant and transfer it into water via a heat exchange unit where it is stored in an insulated tank. This process is driven by a compressor just like an air conditioner and is extremely efficient. A typical system will convert one unit of electricity into three or more units of heat. This is referred to as the coefficient of performance (COP).

Heating water using electricity produced from solar PV has become increasingly practical

---

As part of my research work, I was closely following the increased uptake of heat pumps with solar PV, and was keen to better understand the energy savings and reductions in greenhouse gas emissions compared to the gas-boosted solar thermal system we were using. In 2018, we replaced the old hot-water system with a new heat pump unit as part of a broader upgrade that saw us replace the gas cooktop (see page 85) and disconnect from the gas service. The new unit was located on the ground at the rear of the house where it is close to the hot water uses, but out of the way. Careful

attention was paid to lagging (insulating) the pipes to reduce heat loss, as well as programming the system to run during the middle of the day when adequate solar PV electricity is typically available.

The results have been impressive. Overall, our family uses approximately 1.8 kWh (kilowatt hours) of electricity per day to produce enough hot water for four people. The compressors on heat pumps do make noise, similar to a reverse cycle air conditioning system, so it's important to position them where this won't be a problem for you or your neighbours. Programming to run during the middle of the day has the added benefit of being a time when people are often away from home.

LEFT: Solar hot-water heaters are a good option in many circumstances. Josh originally installed a gas-boosted solar hot-water heater but upgraded to a heat pump after deciding to discontinue using gas.

BELOW: Heat pump hot-water systems can be programmed to run when solar energy is available, or during low-tariff periods.

Josh's 'all electric' home fit-out was complete after installing an induction cooktop.

COOKING

Our original choices of cooking appliances were a gas cooktop and electric oven. In 2012, induction cooktops where comparatively expensive and, given we were already connecting to the reticulated gas network to supply the hot-water system booster, a gas cooktop seemed a sensible selection.

The replacement of the hot-water system with one that didn't require gas made us reconsider our cooktop too. The idea of an all-electric house that ran mostly, if not completely, on solar PV was now in reach. Disconnecting the gas service would also mean one less utility bill to worry about and, like heat pumps, induction cooktops had dramatically come down in price.

The idea of an all-electric house that runs mostly, if not completely, on solar PV is now in reach

---

Cooking using induction cooktops is more energy efficient than using standard electric cooktops. They work by inducing an electric current within the base of a pot or pan, which generates heat through resistance within the cooking surface. This makes the cooking surface highly responsive to changes to the selected temperature and there is less waste heat, so less wasted energy. Cooking vessels such as pots and pans need to be made of materials compatible with induction, through the inclusion of high-ferrous metal in their manufacture, in order to work effectively. We found a new home for our beloved cookware and invested in some induction-compatible pots and pans as part of the cost of the changeover.

We upgraded to an induction cooktop shortly after the heat pump hot-water system went in. Soon after that, we disconnected the gas. On average, we use around 0.6 kWh worth of energy per day for cooking, between the oven and induction, with the induction cooktop representing just under half of that amount.

The open-plan kitchen and dining room at Josh's house is the heart of the house and is naturally well lit and thermally comfortable year-round.

CEILING FANS

Through good passive design, our home is comfortable to live in year-round. In winter, all that is needed is warm clothes and a rug on the couch. In summer, ceiling fans provide the extra bit of comfort needed on hot days, especially when the nights are still.

We installed ceiling fans in all the habitable rooms, including living and dining room, kitchen and bedrooms. Fans complement the body's natural cooling system in a similar way to natural breezes, providing a sense of three degrees in temperature drop. If the room is at an upper limit of 26°C, the fans makes it feel like 23°C, which is considerably more comfortable. Fans use very little energy to operate, and if quality models are chosen and installed properly, they make very little noise. It's a good idea to choose a model with multiple speed settings to provide the appropriate level of comfort for the conditions and have them installed in living areas and bedrooms where they will be best utilised.

In winter, ceiling fans can also be used to circulate warm air that rises to the ceiling around the rest of the room by operating in 'reverse' mode. Our fans have this functionality, but in the time that we've been living in our home, we've never had the need to use it.

Ceiling fans can provide a sense of cooling of 3°C and can make conditions much more comfortable on hot, still days. They are also very economical to run.

ACTIVE HEATING AND COOLING OPTIONS

If additional heating and cooling is required for your home, there are a range of options to choose from.

Reverse Cycle Air Conditioning:
Split systems are considered the most energy-efficient option for heating and cooling specific rooms (up to 100 m²) and will quickly condition the air. Choose a model with minimum 5-star energy efficiency rating and get professional advice on location and system sizing.

Hydronic Heating:
These systems circulate hot water through a closed-loop network of pipes in the slab and/or through radiator panels in specific rooms. The most efficient way to heat the water is via heat pump systems (either air source or ground source), which can also provide hot-water service needs. Hydronic heating is best suited to homes with high thermal mass so that the heat is stored in the slab and walls. Appropriate slab and wall insulation is important so heat doesn't leak from the building. Hydronic cooling using the same principles is also possible, although less common. Slab heating can also be achieved with simple electrical elements, essentially wires, embedded into the slab, but anecdotal reporting on these is that electricity consumption tends to be very high – probably higher than can be practically sourced from a solar PV system. Both hydronic pipework and electric heating elements are embedded into the slab when the concrete is poured and can't be readily retrofitted.

Wood-fired Heating:
Modern wood-combustion heaters with in-built fans can be a very efficient way to heat a home. They are best suited to areas where a steady supply of sustainably sourced wood or wood pellets is available and where they are unlikely to cause nuisance issues from smoke. In urban areas, you should check with your local council about whether wood-fired heating is permitted.

ABOVE & LEFT: Light tubes were installed at Josh's house to allow daylight in areas without windows, including the hallway and the walk-in robe.
BELOW: LEDs provide high-quality light. They are extremely efficient and long-lasting.

LIGHTING

Lighting and appliances account for around a quarter of a typical home's energy load. With the rapid uptake in highly efficient LED lights, it is easier than ever to reduce wastage simply through sensible product choice.

In our home, we selected LED lights for all habitable rooms, and compact fluorescent lights in the hallways, bathrooms and laundry as a cost-saving measure, with the rationale being that we don't spend as much time in these rooms, and the fluorescent light would be suitable for the job. We put the savings into making sure we had good-quality lights that provided excellent light coverage and were dimmable.

The use of sensors can help reduce unnecessary lighting, but in practice, this approach is better suited to commercial buildings than it is in the home. Sensors do play a practical role in outdoor lighting, especially for security.

It is easier than ever to reduce wastage simply through sensible product choice

Just like good design can reduce the need for mechanical heating and cooling to make a home thermally comfortable, good design should also ensure ample natural light enters the home during the day. This not only reduces the need for artificial daytime lighting, but also adds to the feel of a home and improves occupant wellbeing. In our home, the large north-facing windows fill the house with light. The light-coloured walls help to illuminate the spaces, and we have installed light tubes in areas that would otherwise be dark, such as the walk-in robes and the hallway. These devices capture natural light from a lens mounted on the roof and direct it down a reflective tube through the roof cavity, where it lights up a diffuser installed in the ceiling. Essentially, these are a modern take on conventional skylights, and are highly effective.

PLUG-IN APPLIANCES

Plug-in appliances include things like the fridge/freezer, dishwasher, washing machine, clothes dryer, computers and entertainment devices. Australia has the excellent Energy Rating labelling scheme (energyrating.gov.au) to support consumers to make good product choices. The program provides clear labelling on the energy performance of particular appliances, allowing comparisons to be made. More efficient appliances will use less energy and cost less to run. The rating is described in stars (typically 0–6, but some appliances now use a scale of 0–10) and the labelling also provides an indication of energy consumption for typical use expressed in kilowatt hours.

A balance has to be struck when choosing appliances. The highest-rated appliances may come with drawbacks, such as cost, lack of availability or durability concerns. For our dishwasher and front-loading washing machine, for example, we settled on mid-range appliances that were within our budget and had reasonably good energy efficiency ratings of 4 stars. Our other product research via Choice revealed that these appliances were also reasonably well rated for water efficiency at 4.5 stars (see Chapter 6) and performed well for reliability and satisfaction when they were tested against others. With both of these devices, they can be scheduled to operate during the day when solar energy is readily available for use.

It's important to note that occupant behaviour affects appliance energy use and often has a greater impact on energy consumption than the efficiency rating. Running a washing machine or dishwasher less regularly when full rather than at half full will lead to energy savings.

Standby consumption (the amount of energy used when a device is switched on but idle) is also less of a problem than it used to be due to improvements in appliance design. Standby power consumption is typically specified on product labelling or can easily be tested using low-cost power meters (see Chapter 8). You can eliminate standby power by switching appliances off at the wall and appliances can be grouped together on a common power board (such as entertainment devices) so that they can be switched off collectively. A 'green switch' can be installed as part of an electrical system design to turn off non-essential circuits when leaving the house, while leaving on essential circuits that supply power to appliances such as the fridge and alarm system. Note that some 'smart' devices are designed to be left on to enable network communication via the home's internet service.

Industry is on the cusp of a new generation of home device integration where smart home platforms will enable the automated scheduling of appliances based on energy load management and optimisation of available solar energy. To some extent, this functionality already exists with smart home systems that enable the programming of lights, appliances, blinds and other devices, but they are often complicated and expensive for what they actually deliver in terms of performance gain. This is a rapidly moving area and improvements in technology, industry capacity and, ultimately, consumer expectations will likely see greater uptake of automated systems in our homes.

CAR CHARGING

Australia has been slow in taking up electric vehicles (EV) compared to other countries. Despite this, they are coming. It is estimated that by 2025 all major vehicle manufacturers will have electrical vehicles in their product range in Australia, at comparable prices to their internal combustion engine offerings. EV are cheaper to run and often outperform their counterparts. They are quiet, reliable and don't produce on-road emissions. When charged at home (which most will be), they are essentially a big appliance, so it's worthwhile planning them into your home design now.

As part of my research work, we conducted a trial to understand the impact of charging an EV at home, and its implications on the degree of self-supply from our solar PV system (see Chapter 5). We installed a dedicated 40 amp circuit and connected a 9.6 kW AC wall-mounted charging unit. This device can be set to match the charge capacity of a particular electric car, or to charge at a selected rate. In our case, the loan vehicle we were provided had a maximum charging capacity of 3.3 kW (factory set). This capacity, although modest, meant that it was under the 5 kW peak solar energy capacity of our inverter, meaning that at the right time of day, when there was ample sunshine, we could charge the car completely off solar and still have some left over to run the house.

Charging devices like this can also be programmed to run during off-peak times when electricity costs are at their lowest. Charging the EV used on average 2.4 kWh per day, which represented 19% of the daily house energy load. At the end of the twelve-month

trial, I had to return the vehicle; however, we are now planning to buy our own.

At the right time of day, when there was ample sunshine, we could charge the car completely off solar and still have some left over to run the house

---

Regardless of whether you are planning for an EV in the near term, you should allow for it in the design of your electrical wiring installation. At a minimum, include a 15 amp dedicated circuit connected to a power point outlet in the garage. A charging device can be fitted at a later date.

An energy meter has been installed on the electrical circuit supplying the car charger at Josh's house to track the amount of energy used to charge the car.

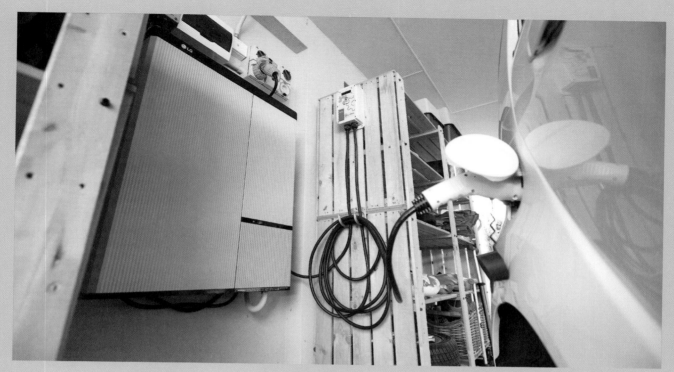

EV CAR CHARGER METER

PERFORMANCE MONITORING

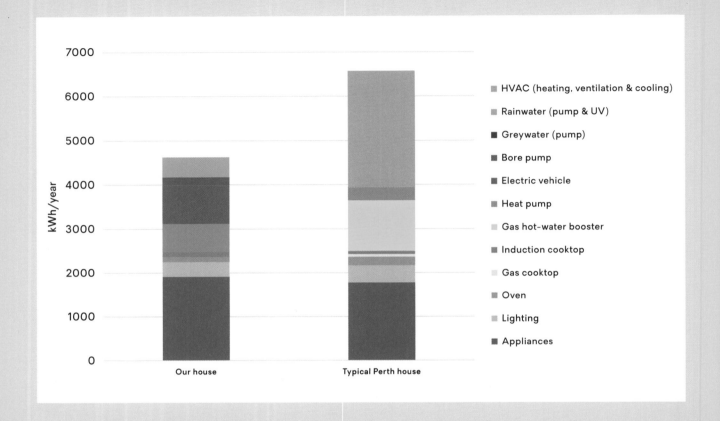

Legend:
- HVAC (heating, ventilation & cooling)
- Rainwater (pump & UV)
- Greywater (pump)
- Bore pump
- Electric vehicle
- Heat pump
- Gas hot-water booster
- Induction cooktop
- Gas cooktop
- Oven
- Lighting
- Appliances

y-axis: kWh/year (0, 1000, 2000, 3000, 4000, 5000, 6000, 7000)

x-axis categories: Our house, Typical Perth house

Energy monitoring at Josh's house shows that it uses 30% less than a typical home, while also accounting for the energy required to pump and treat water and charge an electric vehicle. The major savings come from the fact that Josh's house doesn't require mechanical heating or cooling, which is usually the largest energy demand in a home. Significant savings are also made through the use of an electric heat pump hot-water system over an instantaneous gas unit. The source of energy, and greenhouse gas emission considerations, are discussed in the following chapter.

The hallway light tube provides natural light in a windowless space.

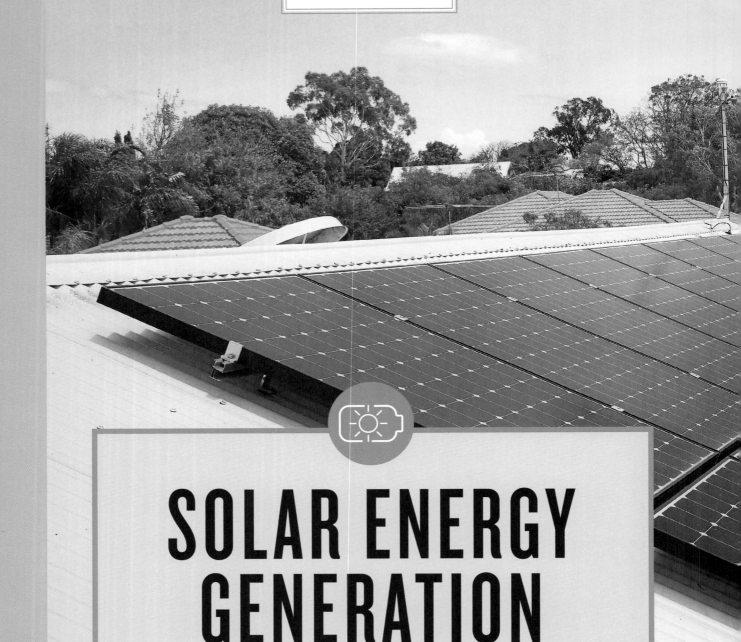

CHAPTER 5

SOLAR ENERGY GENERATION & STORAGE

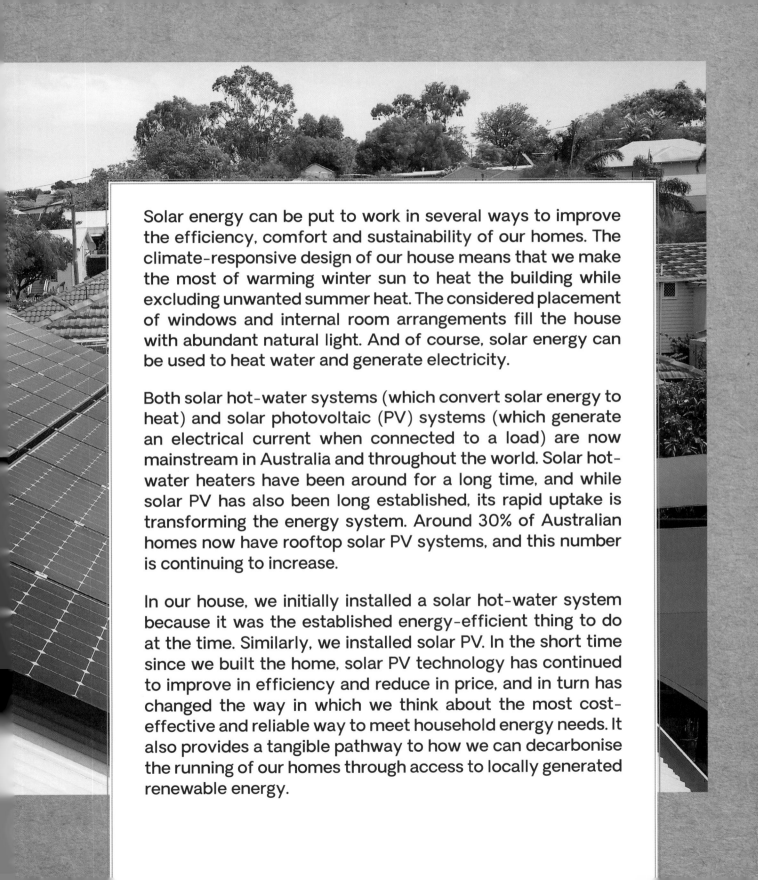

Solar energy can be put to work in several ways to improve the efficiency, comfort and sustainability of our homes. The climate-responsive design of our house means that we make the most of warming winter sun to heat the building while excluding unwanted summer heat. The considered placement of windows and internal room arrangements fill the house with abundant natural light. And of course, solar energy can be used to heat water and generate electricity.

Both solar hot-water systems (which convert solar energy to heat) and solar photovoltaic (PV) systems (which generate an electrical current when connected to a load) are now mainstream in Australia and throughout the world. Solar hot-water heaters have been around for a long time, and while solar PV has also been long established, its rapid uptake is transforming the energy system. Around 30% of Australian homes now have rooftop solar PV systems, and this number is continuing to increase.

In our house, we initially installed a solar hot-water system because it was the established energy-efficient thing to do at the time. Similarly, we installed solar PV. In the short time since we built the home, solar PV technology has continued to improve in efficiency and reduce in price, and in turn has changed the way in which we think about the most cost-effective and reliable way to meet household energy needs. It also provides a tangible pathway to how we can decarbonise the running of our homes through access to locally generated renewable energy.

The solar PV system at Josh's house is located on the north-facing roof for maximum year-round energy production.

SOLAR PV

Photovoltaic panels generate current when exposed to light photons. The technology has been developed over the last century, with grid-connected home PV systems emerging in Australia over the last decade or so. Home solar PV systems are comprised of a solar array (panels) and an inverter which converts direct current (DC) that is generated by the solar panels into alternating current (AC) for use in the home. The inverter also controls the amount of solar-generated electricity that is supplied to the house or exported back to the electricity grid via your utility meter. The generation capacity of a solar PV array is described as kWp, or kilowatt peak, to indicate what the array will produce under ideal conditions. A PV system output will vary depending on solar input, and will naturally change through the day. Inverter capacity is also described in kWp, and this refers to the maximum amount of power the inverter can make available to your home or export to the grid.

Improvements in technology, manufacturing and increased scale of production has meant costs of PV systems continue to come down. Generous rebates in the early years helped support the uptake of systems, where the financials otherwise didn't stack up. These days, while rebates and other incentives do still exist at a federal level in the form of the Small-scale Renewable Energy Scheme (cleanenergyregulator.gov.au), as well as additional incentives provided by some states, the cost of solar PV systems are now at a point where the business case for installing them is driving the uptake. The average system in Australia is now above the 5 kWp mark, with a cost of around $5000 on average after rebates (although much lower in some states due to additional incentives), and a financial payback period of typically under four years through reduced electricity bills. The old argument perpetuated by detractors of solar energy – that the energy required to make these systems outweighs their benefits – is also outdated, with research showing that the energy payback for system manufacture and supply chain is around two to three years. In other words, a typical solar PV system will soon recover its embodied energy cost through renewable energy generation and will be providing genuine clean energy from then on.

> A typical solar PV system will soon recover its embodied energy cost through renewable energy generation

When we built our house, we first installed a 2.5 kWp inverter and a 3 kWp solar PV array. This was sized to cover the net energy needs of our household across the course of a year. In other words, the amount of solar energy produced would meet or exceed the amount of energy used to run the home, including gas used for cooking and for the solar hot-water system booster. This concept is referred to as 'net zero energy' and is a useful benchmark to inform decisions around energy performance and renewable energy system sizing in buildings.

When we decided to upgrade our cooktop and hot-water system to disconnect from reticulated gas, we also upgraded our solar PV system to cover the additional electrical load. At this point, we recalculated the likely energy demand of the home to account for the operational energy requirements of running the house, as well as covering the demand of charging two electric vehicles, using a simple-to-use online tool called PVWatts (pvwatts.nrel.gov/pvwatts.php). Based on this, we opted for a 6.4 kWp solar PV array and a 5 kWp inverter. The 5 kWp inverter sizing was based on it meeting the requirements of our network electricity retailer, where systems up to this size are eligible to receive a solar feed-in tariff for exported energy, whereas larger systems are not (see Box). The oversizing of the PV array relative to the inverter improves the performance of the system during winter months when days are shorter and conditions can be cloudy. In any event, total production is capped at 5 kWp.

The best way to utilise the energy produced from rooftop solar PV is to time the use of appliances to when the energy is available. As discussed in the previous chapter, this works particularly well with electric hot-water heating, which can be timed to heat during the day, as well as appliances that can be scheduled to run during the day, such as dishwashers and washing machines, or the charging of electric vehicles.

A major consideration for rooftop solar PV is locating the panels where they get exposure to maximum sunlight. Shade from trees and other structures should be avoided as this will dramatically affect performance. In all parts of the southern hemisphere, a north-facing aspect will provide the best exposure to sunlight throughout the year, which is how our panels were installed. The angle of the panels is less significant but should be at least 10 degrees, tilted to the north, to self-clean when it rains. If roof design or shading obstruction prohibits locating the panels on the northern aspect, then eastern and western aspects

It's important not to shade solar PV panels. At Josh's house, shade trees and shade structures were carefully chosen and located so as not to impact system performance.

SOLAR FEED-IN TARIFFS

The term 'solar feed-in tariff' (FiT) refers to credits obtained when surplus electricity that has been generated from solar PV installations is exported from a property to the grid. The amount of electricity exported is recorded by the property electricity meter. FiT values vary between states and energy retailers and can change over time. They typically range from around 7 cents to 15 cents per kWh. Some people may still be on early state-government funded FiT that are much higher, although these have limited lifespans and are no longer available to new customers. FiT are administered by energy retailers, who should be contacted directly for specific terms and conditions. Some retailers will pay out the cash value of FiT credits, while others will only allow the credit to be deducted from a current bill. FiT are sometimes referred to as 'solar tariffs' or 'solar buy-back rate'.

can also be used. This can actually be favourable in some circumstances, for example in summer – panels located on the western side of a house are going to receive more direct sunlight in the late afternoon and early evening, which matches well with the operation of air conditioning and other end-of-day electrical loads. The downside is that in winter, in southern parts of the country where the sun is rising and setting in a narrow arc, the panels will receive a lot less direct light.

The residential solar PV market is a crowded and highly competitive space and it can be confusing as to who to go with when installing a system. The first thing to look for is a supplier who is willing to assist you with properly sizing your system, based on your property type and location, roof design and electrical load. The quality of equipment and warranty periods are other things to check. It's best to use reputable brands by recognised manufacturers. Warranty periods will differ between the components. Panels are expected to last 25 years, whereas an inverter will typically last for 10 years. There will also be a separate warranty period for installation, which may only be for 12 months. Using an established company with a good reputation rather than the cheapest option will likely result in better quality trade work and materials used, and will reduce the risk of disappointment.

BATTERIES

The use of home batteries in conjunction with rooftop solar PV is rapidly gaining momentum, with the obvious benefit being that surplus solar energy that is generated during the day can be stored. Until relatively recently, the use of batteries in homes was mainly in situations where back-up power was required, such as in remote areas or regions where the electrical grid is unreliable, and the main battery chemistry was lead-acid types, which are relatively bulky and require ongoing maintenance. A new generation of home batteries based on lithium ion chemistry is now available, and they have the advantage of being more compact and maintenance free. The chemistry is well known, being the same battery type as mobile phones, laptop computers and common power tools.

A new generation of home batteries based on lithium ion chemistry is now available, and they have the advantage of being more compact and maintenance free

---

The pace at which lithium batteries have become available and relatively affordable has caught many by surprise. The rate at which the technology is improving is also impressive and, like solar PV, the expectation is that the scaling up of production will see prices quickly fall to make them a cost-effective option for many households.

We installed our first battery in 2015 as part of a research project to better understand the role that batteries can play in increasing the amount of self-supply of solar electricity in homes. It was the first battery system to be installed on a grid-connected residential property on the Perth regional electricity grid, and it went in when we still had the original 3 kWp solar PV array and 2.5 kW inverter, as well as the gas-boosted solar hot-water system and gas cooktop. The approvals took months and there was only one unit on the market that was both available and met the regulatory criteria for installation.

It was an 8 kWh unit consisting of two cabinets – one of the battery modules and the other for an inverter and energy management system. The bi-directional inverter was required to convert the AC current from the inverter to DC current for storage in the battery, then back to AC again for use in the house. If the battery was full, the AC current from the inverter would bypass the battery and export directly to the grid. If the battery state of charge dropped below a programmed shut-off point of 10%, electricity would be imported from the grid. In the event of a blackout, the battery would provide electricity to the home, with a safeguard in place to prevent export of electricity from the battery to the grid.

Prior to installing the first battery, with the PV system, gas-boosted solar hot-water unit and gas cooktop, our household energy demand was met with 35% self-supply from PV, 53% from grid and 12% from gas. Annual PV export was 3970 kWh, or 78% of total production. Total calculated annual greenhouse gas emissions from household operational energy use was 1157 kg of CO_2-e, which was offset by 140% or 2779 kg of CO_2-e based on exported solar PV electricity.

The battery at Josh's house is located in the garage and neatly wall mounted so it is safely out of the way.

After we installed the first battery, self-supply (PV plus battery) more than doubled, to meet 73% of demand. Greenhouse gas emissions reduced by 71% to 332 kg of CO_2-e, and grid export reduced by 71% to 474 kWh as a result of the increased self-consumption enabled by the battery, plus losses that were attributed to how the battery system operated, also known as 'parasitic load'.

When we upgraded the hot-water system and cooktop to electric appliances in 2018, as well as the solar PV system, we also took the opportunity to upgrade the battery. This was for technical reasons. The original battery had a protection setting that would cause it to trip a circuit breaker if the load exceeded 9 kW. This wasn't an issue in the original configuration; however, adding the electrical load of the induction cooktop (induction cooking draws a large amount of current) and accounting for the charging of an electric vehicle would mean that regular tripping would likely become a nuisance.

The number of batteries that were available on the market and approved for use had increased dramatically even in those three years. The technology had also improved. We chose a unit that could be charged

Hybrid inverters like the one installed at Josh's house are battery ready, meaning they can be installed to operate like a conventional inverter initially, converting DC power generated by solar panels into AC for use in a house and exporting to the grid, and then be configured to operate with a battery at a later date.

directly from the new solar hybrid inverter, which is capable of either sending the DC current generated by the solar panels straight to the battery for charging, or converting it to AC for powering household appliances, and exporting surplus AC electricity to the grid. This new arrangement virtually eliminated the parasitic load issue experienced with the previous battery, charges more quickly and is significantly smaller in size.

With the upgrade to all electric appliances, the annual household operational energy usage increased by around 20% (or 614 kWh), due to the additional running of the heat pump, remembering that, while this is a highly efficient system, it runs entirely on electricity, whereas the solar hot-water system ran on solar thermal input, with gas used only for boosting. The charging of the electric vehicle added a further 19% (or 867 kWh)

to energy consumption. Self-supply was 92%, made up of 54% PV and 38% battery, with the remaining 8% being imported from the grid. Grid import is 367 kWh and export to the grid is 6647 kWh over an average year.

The new battery, like most of the current crop of home energy storage systems, is designed to be grid connected. It does not provide back-up if there is a blackout, and it is not for use in an 'off-grid' system. When we have experienced a blackout with this system in place, both the PV and battery automatically shut off and then come back on again when the grid supply is back up. Home batteries for locations on the grid have become simpler, smaller and less expensive, leaving those other applications to specialised devices.

PERFORMANCE MONITORING

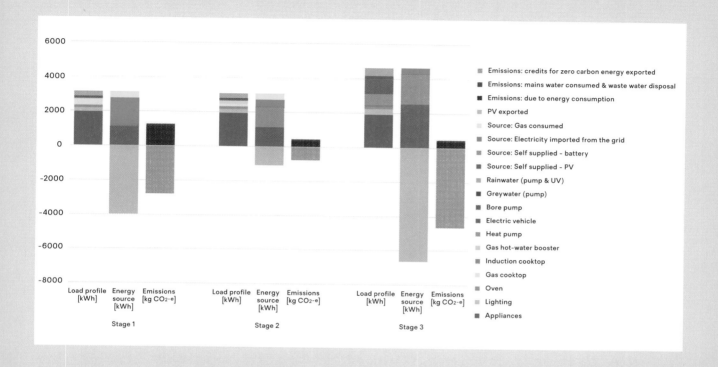

Energy use at Josh's house has been monitored over a number of years to understand the impact of different technologies and energy system configurations on improvements in solar utilisation and reduction in greenhouse gas (GHG) emissions. The introduction of battery storage in 2015 (Stage 2) saw a significant increase in the amount of solar being utilised and less energy required from the grid to run the home.

Further upgrades were undertaken in 2018 (Stage 3) to eliminate the need for natural gas and enable the charging of an electric vehicle (EV). The house now meets its own energy needs most of the time, with grid demand typically associated with EV charging at times when solar is not being generated. Net energy export significantly exceeds grid import along with the associated GHG emissions.

CHAPTER 6

WATER SYSTEMS

Australia is becoming hotter and drier as a result of climate change. Rainfall is becoming more variable, and extreme events such as storms and floods more unpredictable. Large-scale water supply and drainage systems that service our cities and towns are not well adapted to this climatic uncertainty. Water shortages during times of drought and localised flooding following storms are now commonplace and the impact on people and the environment is significant.

My thinking on urban water management has been shaped by responding to the reality of a drying climate. In my early researching career, and as a keen gardener, I observed the drying of Perth's climate and the introduction of permanent water-saving measures. I closely followed the response to the Millennium drought on the east coast, which saw rapid implementation of water-saving measures during that first decade, only to see many dismissed once the drought broke.

While we can't make it rain or stop violent storms, we can design our homes and suburbs to be more resilient to an uncertain climate and reduce the pressure on costly city-scale water infrastructure. At our house, we implemented initiatives to reduce demand on precious drinking water, ranging from efficient appliances through to using alternative sources such as rainwater, greywater and sustainably managed groundwater. The result has been a 90% reduction when compared to the typical mains water consumption in Perth, while maintaining a beautiful, productive and shady garden.

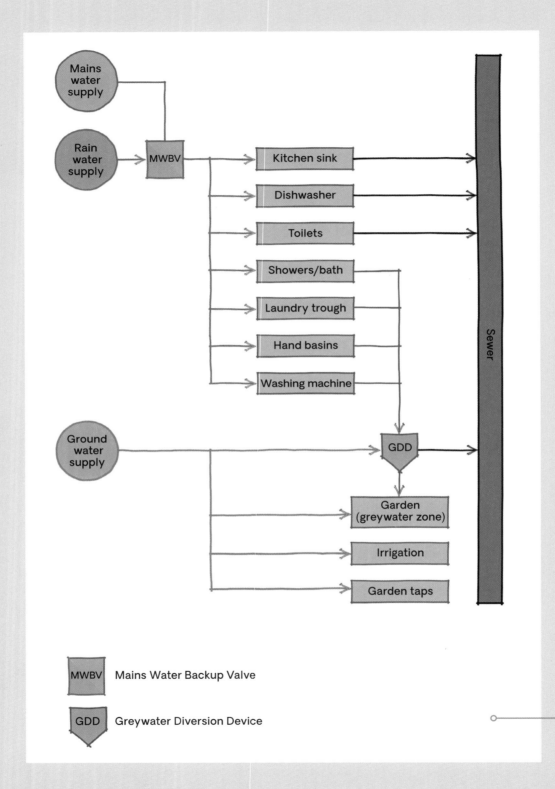

FIXTURES AND APPLIANCES

Good water management begins with efficient use of water, and selecting water-efficient fixtures and appliances is the best place to start. In Australia, we have the federally regulated Water Efficiency Labelling and Standards (WELS) scheme (waterrating.gov.au), which makes it easy to compare water usage between similar products in the same way as the Energy Rating labelling scheme can be used to compare the energy efficiency of electrical appliances (see Chapter 4). Ratings are described in stars (0–6), and the typical volume of water usage is provided. Things like shower heads and taps are described in litres per minute (L/min). Toilets are described as litres per flush, with full flush and half flush volumes specified. Washing machines and dishwashers are described in litres per wash. All of the fixtures and appliances are required by law to be rated prior to sale or supply and some states mandate efficiency requirements.

The volumetric usage will typically have a range within a defined WELS star band. For example, 3-star shower heads, which is currently recognised as the highest star rating, include those with flow rates up to nine litres per minute, but can be significantly lower. At our house, we installed a 6.5 L/min shower head in the en suite, which is still considered 3-star. In the main bathroom, we installed a 9 L/min shower head, which is also classified 3-star. We went for this 9 L/min model as, at the time, it was the most efficient shower head with a hand-held nozzle, which we felt was practical for small children.

Efficient fixtures such as this 6.5 L/min shower head help to reduce water use.

Josh's house is serviced by several water sources including rainwater, mains water and groundwater, and greywater is collected and used for garden irrigation. This schematic diagram shows the flow path of water from the various sources and how it is used.

Both of our toilets have a 4.5 L full flush and a 3 L half flush. The main toilet includes an integrated handbasin so that when you flush, you can wash your hands with clean water before it refills the toilet cistern. Effectively, the water is used twice. As a result, this toilet is rated at 5-star, whereas the other is rated at 4-star. Our handbasin taps are rated at 5-star, with a flow rate of 6 L/min, and the kitchen sink and laundry taps are 4-star at 7.5 L/min. The dishwasher has a rating of 4.5-star using 12.8 L per wash, and the front-loading washing machine has a 4.5-star rating and uses 60 L per wash.

Low water–use fixtures and appliances are only half of the water efficiency story. The other part is water-efficient behaviour. Keeping showers short, turning off taps when not needed and fully filling the washing machine and dishwasher prior to use all add up to water savings.

RIGHT: The main toilet at Josh's house has the handbasin integrated with the cistern. When flushed, clean water runs through the faucet for hand washing, which then fills the cistern to be reused to flush the toilet.

RAINWATER HARVESTING

Rainwater harvesting involves collecting rain that falls on the roof and storing it for later use. In many parts of the country, it's an effective way to reduce reliance on mains water, provided the use is seasonally practical, that is, rainwater is available when you need to use it, and the water quality is safe to use for the intended purpose. Many rural and remote properties require complete self-sufficiency when it comes to rainwater capture if no mains water connection is available.

Our house has an 18,000 L steel tank, with a food-grade flexible liner, connected to 200 m² of roof catchment. We use this water to supply indoor needs. Rain is collected in gutters and directed into downpipes fitted with screens designed to exclude leaves and insects from the tank to protect water quality and prevent pest problems.

The downpipes and tank have been configured as a 'charged' rainwater collection system, which means that all the stormwater pipes between the gutters and tank inlet are permanently full of water. To eliminate the potential of the rainwater in the pipes becoming stagnant during dry weather periods, a diversion valve has been fitted below ground to discharge this unwanted water into a large soakwell that has been constructed from modular recycled plastic drainage cells and is located under the driveway. By leaving this valve open, the 'first flush' of rain containing dust and

The 18,000 L steel rainwater tank is a feature in the landscape at Josh's house, with the water used inside the home.

other contaminants which build up on the roof surface during dry weather is discarded. The overflow from the tank is also directed to the soakwell, where it infiltrates into the ground to recharge an underlying aquifer.

We use a pressure switch pump to deliver the water from the tank to the house, which kicks in when water is drawn on. We have also included a 90 L pressure vessel, which is a small metal tank that contains a rubber bladder filled with air that becomes compressed when the tank fills with the water. The vessel stores approximately 45 L of water under pressure and is connected to the supply line between the pump and the various fixtures and appliances that draw water, reducing the number of times that the pump has to run, saving both energy and pump wear and tear. The pump also has an automatic cut-off switch if the water supply is interrupted, to prevent the pump from running dry and getting damaged.

Water pressure and flow rate are important considerations when choosing a pump. We selected a model capable of supplying 70 L/min at 300 kPa, which is suitable for our home, being single storey and using low flow rate fixtures. Two-storey homes, or homes with specific high flow rate requirements, such as firefighting, would likely need a larger pump. Alternatively, a smaller pump would be suitable if only supplying rainwater for non-potable demands such as toilet flushing, washing machine and garden tap use, which is a more common scenario in urban settings. In this situation, a separate water supply line (dual plumbing) supplies these demands from the tank, and mains water supplies the rest of the house and provides a back-up to the tank supply. In urban settings, if using an above-ground pump, locate it in a position where it won't annoy neighbours, or consider installing an acoustic cover. Submersible pumps are inherently less of an issue because the water they are surrounded in eliminates most of the noise.

As we use the rainwater we collect for indoor purposes, including drinking and cooking, we treat the water with filtration and ultraviolet (UV) disinfection. The filtration is a two-stage process. The first filter has a 20-micron (µm) grade cartridge which removes sediment and other particles, and the second filter has a 1-µm grade cartridge which removes parasitic cysts that are resistant to UV, and ultrafine particles that can shield organisms from UV. The UV disinfection lamp sterilises the water by killing pathogenic microorganisms.

The rainwater we collect supplies our in-house water needs for about eight months of the year

---

The rainwater we collect supplies our in-house water needs for about eight months of the year. Perth has a Mediterranean winter-wet, summer-dry climate type where rain usually falls from May through to around October. During this period, the tank is continually topped up and drawn on for use. Once the rain stops, the tank is gradually emptied, with the stored water typically lasting through to early January. When the rainwater runs out, mains water is automatically supplied via a mains water backup valve – a commonly available device that is fitted after the pump and has both the rainwater and mains water connected to it. The model we installed uses a float switch (which is installed in the tank) to determine if rainwater is available for pumping. If the float switch indicates that the tank is empty, mains water is supplied. Mains water is also supplied automatically in the event of a pump failure.

LEFT: Leaf screens installed between the gutter and the downpipes keep leaves, debris and insects out of the tank.
BOTTOM LEFT: Rainwater pipe work is typically coloured green in line with national plumbing standards.
BOTTOM RIGHT: Large rainwater tanks are typically assembled on site.

RAINWATER TANK OPTIONS

There is a large variety of rainwater storage options on the market, from both materials and application perspectives. The main options for standard tanks include 'poly', steel and concrete.

Poly Tanks: Made from UV-stabilised food-grade polyethylene, they tend to be the cheapest option for tanks under 5000 L. These tanks are also lightweight for ease of transportation and installation. Most manufacturers will guarantee poly tanks for 10 years. They are commonly available in round or narrow profile in a range of colours. Poly tanks can be sited on a level, compacted bed of free-draining sand.

Steel Tanks: Typically fabricated from corrugated steel sheeting coated with a polymer film on the inside for durability and water quality. Steel tanks can either be round or narrow profile and are available in a range of colours, including the classic galvanised look. The warranty on the materials can be as long as 20 years (depending on the product); however, the warranty on workmanship is often significantly less and should be clarified when comparing prices. Prefabricated steel tanks must be sited on a level, firm base, such as a specified stand, concrete slab or sturdy paving, with this requirement usually specified as part of the warranty. Steel tanks over 25,000 L are assembled on site and have flexible food-grade liners to keep them watertight.

Concrete Tanks: Often used when large underground storage is required. They can either be transported to site or made in situ, depending on the size and site access. Depending on the construction style, concrete tanks may require lining, which can come in the form of a flexible liner or paint-on sealant. In situ tanks are often poured with a sealing agent mixed into the concrete so they are watertight once set.

Where space is not an issue, round, above-ground tanks are the most cost-effective option. Narrow-profile tanks are ideal for siting alongside walls and under eaves. Where space is particularly tight, tanks can be installed underground. This is the costliest option as the tanks must be structurally engineered to cope with the load of the surrounding soil, as well as whatever is placed on top of them – including vehicles if they are being placed in a trafficable area. The cost of installing underground tanks will vary depending on the local geology and access for excavation equipment. Bladders designed to be laid under decking, or under floorboards between joists, are also available, but this is a relatively expensive option compared to above-ground tanks.

Source: Byrne, J. (2013), Small Space Organics, Hardie Grant Books, Melbourne

Matching time of use and time of rainfall with the aim of only storing enough rainwater to provide reliable supply is a practical compromise when space is limited

We are often asked why we didn't put in a bigger tank to store enough water to meet our needs throughout the year. The answer is simple – it would take up too much space. Matching time of use and time of rainfall with the aim of only storing enough rainwater to provide reliable supply is a practical compromise when space is limited and mains water is available for backup, as is the case in cities. For us to store enough rainwater for 12 months indoor usage, we would need to increase the storage to around 50,000 L. If we didn't have access to groundwater for irrigation and wanted to maintain the same garden using rainwater, then our tank would have to be around 140,000 L. Conversely, if we were only looking to use rainwater for toilet flushing and washing machine use (which is the most common and requires no treatment) and be satisfied with rainwater only being available during the rainy periods, then a 3000 L tank would have been adequate. The point is that there are practical limitations with rainwater harvesting based on rainfall, available space for storage and cost. There are useful on-line calculators (tankulator.ata.org.au) that can assist with sizing tanks based on location (rainfall patterns), roof area (catchment size), occupancy and uses (demand) and these should be used to inform your decisions.

Collecting rainwater to supply all indoor uses, like we do, does take some maintenance to make sure the system works reliably, and the water quality is fit for purpose. We make sure the gutters are cleaned before autumn rains arrive, check that downpipe screens are clear of leaves and other debris, and replace the cartridge filters and UV lamp every 12 months. Because our tank is protected from foreign material entering it through the use of screens and diversion of dirty water, there is no need to clean it out.

Greywater pipework is typically coloured purple in line with national plumbing standards. Here, the purple dripline distributing greywater has been installed in a garden bed and will be covered with mulch.

GREYWATER REUSE

Greywater is household wastewater that hasn't come into contact with toilet wastewater. This includes shower, bath, laundry and handbasin water, which can be safely applied to the garden, including many native plants, through appropriate reuse systems and careful selection of detergents and cleaning products. Kitchen and dishwasher wastewater is typically excluded because it contains food scraps, fats and oils which can cause clogging of greywater system filters and drippers, as well as harsh detergents which can impact soil and plant health.

On average in Australia, we produce around 100 L of greywater per person per day, so a family of four could expect to produce around 400 L per day, which is enough to irrigate 40–60 m² of high water–use garden, or more if low water–use plants are used. Reusing greywater takes the pressure off precious scheme water resources and provides a valuable source of household irrigation water that is not limited by restrictions.

Greywater Regulations

The legalities of greywater reuse are managed on a state-by-state basis, and while it is permitted in all states, the approval process differs slightly, as do the specifics of how it can be used. That said, local requirements are typically based on national wastewater standards and plumbing codes, so the example of what we have done at our house is relevant to other regions around the country, as are the safety and management suggestions provided (see Box on page 124).

In WA, the requirements for approved greywater reuse are outlined in a Department of Health Code of Practice, which details the approvals process and greywater irrigation considerations such as the required setbacks from property boundaries and paths for greywater application, greywater application rates and greywater dispersal area calculations. Approvals for the installation and operation of greywater systems are managed by local government and all plumbing work must be done by a licensed plumber. The best place to find out more information about the requirements in other states around Australia is via local government environmental health officers, who can advise on local codes and resources.

Types of Greywater Systems

Greywater systems range from simple 'direct diversion' types for reuse on the garden through to advanced 'treatment' types for supplying water to garden taps, toilets and washing machines. Direct diversion systems are the most common. They consist of a mechanism to conveniently divert the greywater from the source to the garden and may also include a surge tank to temporarily store the water, a pump to distribute the water, and a filter to remove material such as hair and lint. With direct diversion systems, greywater must be applied below the surface of the soil via a slotted drain, or under mulch using drip irrigation so that human or animal contact with the greywater is avoided.

Greywater treatment systems are more complicated because they involve treating the water to a point where it is suitable for uses beyond irrigation, or where greater flexibility of irrigation is required and close human contact is likely. Treatment can involve a range of processes depending on the technology used and the water quality requirements of the intended use. Common methods include media filtration, biological digestion and ultrafiltration, as well as disinfection through either chlorination, ozone or ultraviolet light. The design and installation of approved greywater treatment systems, and their ongoing operation, are subject to approvals that are typically administered by local councils. They are considerably more expensive than the simpler direct diversion systems and, depending on the treatment method, can have high operational energy requirements. For these reasons, we opted for a direct diversion type for our house.

GREYWATER QUALITY MANAGEMENT

Greywater reuse is safe provided some basic precautions are taken. The main thing is to avoid direct contact with untreated greywater by irrigating under mulch, by excluding pets and poultry from areas being irrigated with greywater, and by washing your hands after contact. It's also best not to water ground-dwelling veggies and herbs with greywater, particularly those that are consumed raw, because of the risk of ingesting pathogens. Fruit trees and vine crops are fine provided there is no contact between the greywater and the part of the plant that is eaten.

Greywater quality can vary dramatically depending on the type of detergents and cleaning products used in a home. Products that contain chemicals such as bleaching and brightening agents, synthetic fragrances and dyes can have a negative impact on soil health, as can sodium, which is commonly found in powdered washing detergents. There are many 'greywater suitable' cleaning and personal care products available which are typically formulated using plant-based ingredients to minimise impact on garden health and the receiving environment. However, it's important to note that most detergents are alkaline, regardless of their biodegradability, which can increase soil pH and can cause some plants to develop nutrient deficiencies after extended periods of application. Resting the soil by switching off the greywater when it is not needed can help reduce this occurring, along with maintaining healthy, biologically active soil with plenty of added organic matter. Specific nutrient deficiencies can be addressed by applying trace elements to affected plants. If you need to use bleaches and other similar products, divert the greywater to the sewer rather than having it go to the garden.

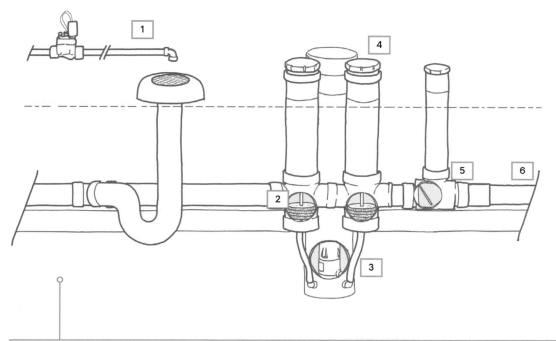

The greywater system at Josh's house is a direct diversion type that irrigates a specific zone in the garden as greywater is generated. The greywater collection pipework and pump-pit unit were installed along with the rest of the wastewater drainage plumbing early in the house construction phase. The pump, controls and irrigation equipment were installed during landscaping works.

1. Top-up water source via an overflow relief gully
2. Filter pad
3. Submersible pump
4. Inspection riser with lid
5. Reflux valve
6. Bypass/overflow to sewer

System Pre-plumbing and Set-up

Whether you choose a direct diversion or treatment system, wastewater drainage plumbing will need to be installed so that greywater can be captured without contamination from toilet and kitchen wastewater. This needs to be agreed with the builder early. This work is not complicated, but it does add costs above standard drainage plumbing due to the additional materials and labour required, and typically ranges between $1000–$2000, depending on house size and layout as well as location and number of greywater sources. If you are planning to install a greywater system with a pump, then you will also need to allow for an outdoor electrical power point.

At our house, we installed a direct diversion greywater system because we have use for the water in the garden throughout the year except for winter, when it is switched off. The system consists of two intercepting traps where greywater passes through coarse polyethylene filter pads and collects in a small sump containing a submersible pump which is activated by a float switch. A reflux valve was also installed to

TOP LEFT: Drainage plumbing needs to be configured to collect greywater separately from toilet and kitchen wastewater.
TOP RIGHT: The greywater system 'Builders Kit' installed during early plumbing works.
BOTTOM LEFT: Top view of the 'Builders Kit' once backfilled and fitted out with pump, filters pads and pipework.
BOTTOM RIGHT: Metering arrangement for monitoring greywater volumes.

prevent the sewer water coming back into the greywater system in the event of back charge. When the pump is running, greywater is delivered to the garden via 25 mm polyethylene pipe and distributed on to garden beds through dripline irrigation. The unit has an automatic filter backflush function, where air is blown through the filters and directed to the sewer, reducing the need for manual filter cleaning. If the pump is switched off, or in the event of a malfunction, the greywater continues to flow along the drainage pipe, past the reflux valve and into the sewer.

The system also has a very practical two-stage set-up process, which begins with the installation of the sump and dual interceptor unit (referred to as the 'Builder's Kit') as well as the reflux valve as part of the initial house drainage plumbing works, followed by the installation of the pump, controls and irrigation piping at a later stage during landscaping. This greatly simplifies the process for making a house 'greywater ready'.

Greywater Irrigation

The size of the greywater system irrigation area is based on the estimated 400 L of greywater generated per day – from the bathroom and laundry – by our household of four. Irrigation rates, like rainfall, are measured in millimetres: 1 mm over 1 m^2 equates to 1 L. Our soil type is very sandy and free-draining, which is suited to an application rate of 10 mm per day (or 10 L) over an area of 40 m^2 of garden incorporating fruit trees, shrubs and other ornamental plantings. The application rate for heavier soil will be lower to prevent the greywater from ponding and will be subject to local requirements.

The greywater is disbursed via purple-coloured substrata dripline irrigation, which is installed on the surface of the soil and covered with a thick layer of mulch. The purple colour of the dripline is an industry standard intended to reduce the likelihood of cross-connection with other water pipework. Likewise, people can instantly identify the pipe as carrying wastewater and know that they should wash their hands after coming into contact with it.

The dripline has holes (drippers) spaced at 300 mm intervals along the length and the driplines are spaced at 300 mm apart to provide uniform distribution on sandy soils. The drippers have a large opening to reduce clogging and are designed to be self-flushing. The dripline is installed between a supply pipe and a collector pipe, and a manual flush valve has been fitted to the collector pipes on each bed to allow for the occasional flushing of the irrigation lines to clear out any muck that accumulates. A vacuum breaker valve has also been included at the highest point of the irrigation line. This allows air to enter through the one-way valve as the water drains out of the line, avoiding the potential for dirt being sucked back through the drippers and blocking them. These components are standard features of a complete drip irrigation system and, if properly installed, will ensure the system performs reliably over time.

Storing untreated greywater is not permitted as it can lead to odours and other issues. With the exception of systems with surge tanks, which can temporarily hold greywater for up to 24 hours (some states only), direct diversion devices will immediately divert greywater when it is generated. If no greywater is being produced in the house, then the garden won't get watered. Regulations prohibit connecting mains water directly to the greywater irrigation system to prevent contamination of the mains water supply. To overcome this, we

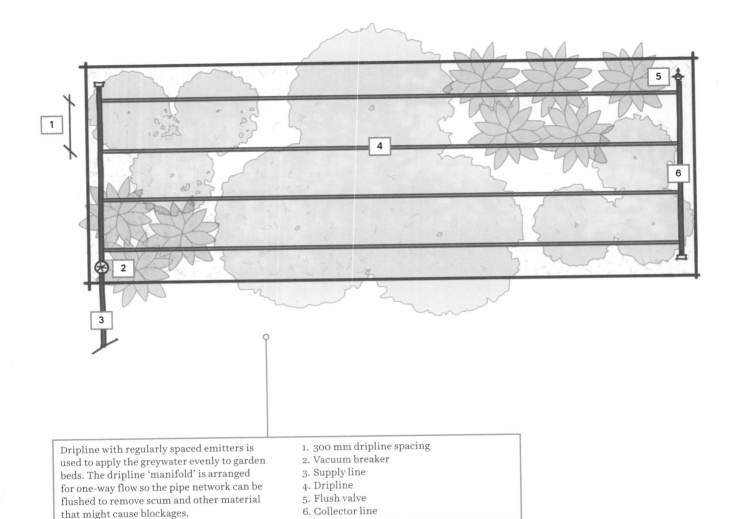

Dripline with regularly spaced emitters is used to apply the greywater evenly to garden beds. The dripline 'manifold' is arranged for one-way flow so the pipe network can be flushed to remove scum and other material that might cause blockages.

1. 300 mm dripline spacing
2. Vacuum breaker
3. Supply line
4. Dripline
5. Flush valve
6. Collector line

installed a top-up line from our main irrigation system (bore water) which delivers water to the greywater drainage pipe via an overflow relief (ORG) gully prior to the greywater system. ORGs are installed on plumbing drainage lines to provide an overflow point in the event of a sewer blockage. They sit just above ground level outside and provide a convenient point to top up a greywater system. The top-up line should sit above the ORG with a clear air gap so there can be no contact between the pipe and sewerage if there is an overflow event. Having this top-up line operated by a solenoid (electromechanical) valve connected to the bore irrigation controller means that it can be programmed to provide water if we are away on holiday. When water flows down the greywater line and into the diversion system, the greywater pump is triggered to come on and the water is directed to that part of the garden.

ON-SITE WASTEWATER SYSTEMS
FOR UNSEWERED SITES

In sewered areas, which includes most of our cities and towns, it is typically a requirement for a house to connect to the reticulated sewerage network to dispose of wastewater, with greywater reuse allowed only. On unsewered sites, such as in rural or peri-urban areas, an on-site wastewater system will be required to treat wastewater that is generated from the house and discharge it within the property. These systems vary from simple septic tank and leach drain systems through to advanced water treatment systems that produce water suitable for landscape irrigation. Like greywater reuse systems, their design must be done in accordance with national standards and plumbing codes and approval for their installation and operation is typically the responsibility of the local council.

A number of factors need to be considered when choosing an on-site wastewater system for your property, including dwelling size, property area, soil type and whether you need the water for irrigation. In some cases, the planning approval for a property might specify the type of system to be used, such as those with advanced nutrient removal if the site is close to sensitive aquatic environments. For these reasons, it is important to seek expert advice early, and your local council is a good place to start for a list of approved systems used in the area, along with any relevant conditions relating to approvals.

Composting toilets, which process toilet waste via aerobic composting, are a good option for unsewered areas, with their use typically restricted to larger sites. Their main advantage is the water savings as most models don't require flushing, as well as the fact that they don't produce a liquid effluent which can be problematic to deal with in some environments. The compost is a bonus too. Once again, your local council is the best place to start regarding the applicability of these systems to your location.

The driveway at Josh's house has been designed to capture stormwater and support healthy plant growth.

STORMWATER INFILTRATION AND GROUNDWATER USE FOR IRRIGATION

Stormwater is rainfall that hits the ground. In urban areas where the ground surface is largely impervious from being covered in materials such as asphalt, concrete and paving, stormwater flows are typically directed to drainage basins and receiving waterways to prevent flooding. In the process, stormwater collects pollutants, such as nutrients from fertiliser, and hydrocarbons from car tyres, oil and fuel residues. Intercepting stormwater close to where it falls slows the transportation of these contaminants and reduces the size of downstream infrastructure required to mitigate flooding. Enabling stormwater to infiltrate the ground also helps support deep-rooted vegetation, which in turn helps to shade and cool the surrounding environment.

In Perth, the sandy soil of the Swan Coastal Plain makes it relatively easy to deal with stormwater on-site. However, the standard approach is to direct stormwater from paved areas into soakwells, along with rainwater collected from roofs. Our garden, on the other hand, has been designed to act like a sponge. Paving has been kept to a minimum and, instead, we've favoured permeable surfaces that allow rain to quickly penetrate to replenish soil moisture to sustain plants and recharge the underlying aquifer which we rely on for irrigation. The deep sandy soils of Perth and access to groundwater are relatively unique when compared to other cities around Australia, but the benefits of reducing stormwater run-off and making the most of this resource is universal.

RAIN GARDENS

In areas with heavy soil and low water permeability, 'rain gardens' are a good option to capture and treat stormwater within the landscape. Rain gardens come in different shapes and sizes, but the basic principle is to direct stormwater flows to a point where it can be detained and percolate through planting media that supports vegetation. They can be made in-ground or as raised planters, and the media should be porous enough to allow the water to infiltrate into the root zone so plants can make the most of the moisture. The design of rain gardens should allow for heavy flows to either bypass or overflow to stormwater drainage to avoid flooding. Benefits from these systems include moisture capture and treatment of light stormwater flows that result from regular, low-volume rain events, and the slowing of water in urban catchments to ease pressure on stormwater infrastructure. They can make great landscape features too.

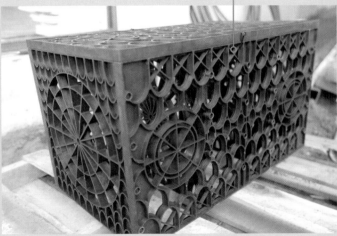

TOP LEFT: Flat plastic drainage cells and geotextile fabric have been laid under the gravel to provide a firm surface for the driveway while allowing water to pass through.
BOTTOM LEFT: Drainage cell detail.
BOTTOM RIGHT: Rectangular drainage cells have been used to create a large soakwell under the driveway to receive the overflow water from the rainwater tank.
RIGHT PAGE: Gravel paths have been used throughout the garden to allow stormwater to pass through.

At our house, we've used several types of permeable surface treatments (outside of planted areas), including decking with spacing between the boards to allow water through, as well as pine bark and gravel paths. We also used gravel for the driveway. To make this suitable for vehicle traffic, lightweight recycled plastic drainage cells were installed to make the surface secure while minimising compaction. The cells lock together and were installed over a geotextile fabric liner that allows water through but prevents the drainage cell and gravel from sinking into the sand. The drainage cells were then filled and covered with locally sourced coarse gravel. In addition to allowing water to penetrate, the gravel driveway was quick to install (taking less than a day), was similar in cost to mid-range paving and looks great. We can also hear people coming as they walk towards the house.

Enabling stormwater to infiltrate the ground helps support deep-rooted vegetation, which in turn helps to shade and cool the surrounding environment

ABOVE: The garden taps are supplied by bore water and are labelled 'not for drinking'.
BOTTOM LEFT & RIGHT: The bore includes an isolation valve and a meter to monitor usage.

Garden Bore

In many parts of Perth's Swan Coastal Plain, groundwater from the superficial aquifer – that closest to the surface – is easily accessible and is generally of suitable quality for garden irrigation (see Box). This groundwater is recharged by winter rainfall and, provided that extraction doesn't exceed infiltration, it can be managed in a sustainable way. In this instance, bore water provides an appropriate fit-for-purpose water source for local food production (where greywater may not be appropriate) and other plants, as opposed to relying on constrained mains water. We can also supply the bore water at a lower energy cost (and carbon cost) than our state water utility can supply mains water, factoring the amount of energy required to produce the water, including treatment and pumping. This is particularly significant in Perth, where desalinated seawater makes up around 50% of our mains water supply. It is a very energy-intensive water source, and its contribution to Perth's mains water supply makeup will continue to increase.

We installed the bore in a non-trafficable section of the driveway to a depth of 30 m. We use the bore water to irrigate the vegetable garden, pots, turf, trees and native plantings (when they need it), and as a back up to the greywater irrigation zone when we are away. The garden taps are also connected to the bore for hand watering, meaning that no mains water is used outside.

Just like with the rainwater system, correct pump selection is critically important for bores to ensure reliable water supply and reduce energy use. We chose a variable speed submersible pump that can provide consistent pressure in response to varying water demands as this allowed us to service different garden

SUSTAINABILITY OF GROUNDWATER USE

It's important to note that the sustainability of groundwater use is highly dependent on the location and nature of the aquifer. In Perth, for example, there are groundwater-sensitive areas across the Swan Coastal Plain where bores aren't appropriate or have been historically overused – the WA Department of Water and Environmental Regulation's Perth Groundwater Atlas (water.wa.gov.au/idelve/gwa) is a useful resource to assist in determining where bores are likely to be suitable. In other regions, advice can be sought from the relevant water resource agency. In Perth, use of groundwater for garden irrigation is restricted to three times per week from September to May, with no irrigation allowed over winter as a way of managing its use and preventing overextraction.

irrigation zones of varying sizes and different emitter types (see Chapter 7) with great flexibility. A pressure sensor located on the mainline connected to the bore pump registers a signal and feeds it to a control unit, which is in turn connected to the pump. The control unit adjusts the pump speed to meet the selected pressure. We have the pressure set at 250 kPa. Whether the bore irrigation system is running a small station of pot drippers, or the entire veggie garden, the pump will ramp up or down to supply the required flow rate (within its operating range) at this pressure. Because the pump doesn't have to work harder than needed for a particular task, there is less wear and tear and it uses less power.

The bore mainline is continually pressurised and runs from the borehole down our driveway to the vegetable garden area and was installed by an irrigation contractor during the landscaping phase. A series of solenoid valves are connected to it at various points along the line and each of these services a particular 'hydrozone' in the garden (see Chapter 7). The valves are connected to a wire cable that runs back to an irrigation controller to allow for the programming of irrigation times specific to each zone. The controller can be accessed remotely via a smart device app to adjust the setting and receive alerts in case of a malfunction. The system receives local weather information via an internet connection and adjusts the irrigation run times based on estimated garden water needs. There is also a rain sensor connected to the controller that switches off the irrigation in the event of rainfall.

We designed our garden on the basis that on average, using a recent annual rainfall figure that is indicative of Perth's drying climate, more stormwater should infiltrate into the ground from our property than we draw from the aquifer for irrigation. This 'water balance' was used to

SHARED WATER SCHEMES

In some new developments, shared non-drinking water schemes are provided where the water is sourced from a community bore, stormwater harvesting or district-scale recycled water scheme.

These are becoming more common as the importance of sustainable water management is being recognised by both industry and government. Shared schemes often mean less maintenance for users and are typically more cost-effective due to efficiencies of scale, while still meeting the goal of reducing reliance on high-quality drinking water for lower order uses.

When choosing a location to build, the availability of a shared non-drinking water scheme should be viewed as desirable.

inform how we allocated water to landscape hydrozones (explained in the following chapter). We also meter our bore to ensure that we are managing it responsibly.

ABOVE: The irrigation controller is located in a safe location in the garden shed.

LEFT: The irrigation system can be managed via an app, making it easy to check water use, adjust programs or test valves.

PERFORMANCE MONITORING

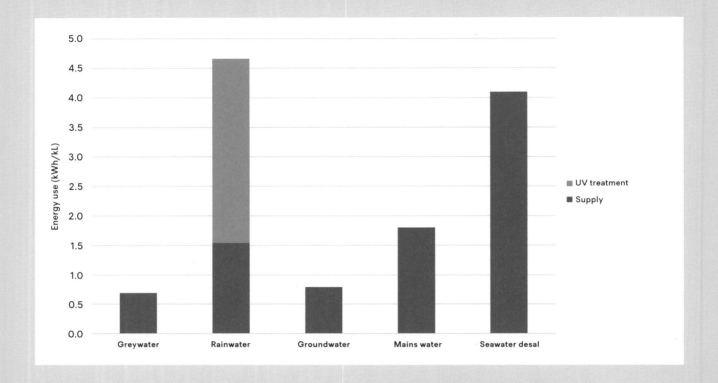

Energy Intensity of Water Sources

The energy intensity of water refers to the amount of energy required to supply water and is described in kWh/kL. Energy metering undertaken at Josh's house shows that greywater and bore water can be supplied at a lower energy cost than mains water from the local utility, and significantly lower than seawater desalination, which is the major water source for Perth. The energy requirement for disinfecting the rainwater using UV (recommended for potable uses) adds to the cost and this has been factored into the sizing of the home's solar energy system to ensure its operation is covered by renewable energy.

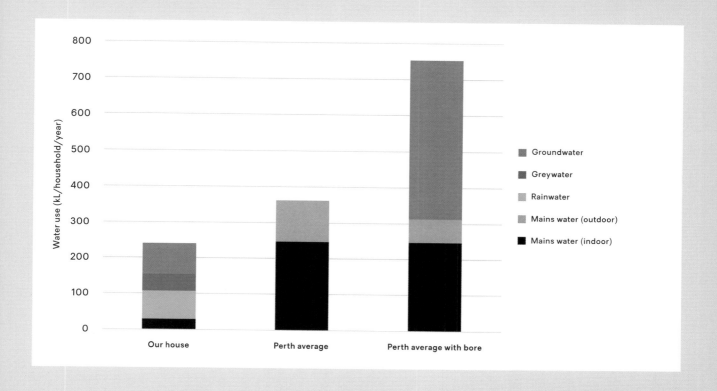

Water use (kL/household/year)

Legend:
- Groundwater
- Greywater
- Rainwater
- Mains water (outdoor)
- Mains water (indoor)

X-axis: Our house | Perth average | Perth average with bore

Water Usage by Source

Data collection at Josh's house shows a 90% reduction in mains water use compared to comparable households in his area. The savings can be attributed to a combination of water-efficiency measures, as well as the incorporation of alternative water sources, including rainwater, greywater and groundwater. Importantly, Josh's house uses significantly less groundwater than the Perth average with a bore, and usage is managed in line with expected recharge rates.

CHAPTER 7

LANDSCAPE

For me, the garden is just as important as the house when it comes to creating a sustainable home. This goes beyond my love of gardening – how the outdoor spaces around a house can have a major impact on building thermal performance is a fundamental design principle. The materials we choose to landscape with come with an environmental cost, just like those that are used to build the house, so careful choices need to be made to reduce impact where possible. Gardens can also support biodiversity and be used for food production, and they can either be water guzzlers or water efficient and in tune with the bioregion and climate.

A well-designed garden also adds to the liveability of a home. Thoughtful relationships between indoor and outdoor spaces need to be considered early, and the garden should suit the occupants' interests and lifestyle just as much as the building. As house blocks become smaller, good design has become increasingly important to make the most of limited outside space to add to the comfort and value of your home.

Our garden has often been described as eclectic because of all the things it contains. Productive gardens, native plantings, play spaces, habitat features and ornamental plantings all combine to make up a garden that reflects my family's interests and hobbies. But there is 'systems thinking' that underpins the inclusion and positioning of the various features and elements, one that draws on permaculture design, and the considerations of resource efficiency and recycling across the property and beyond.

Outdoor spaces at Josh's house have been designed to work as an extension of the home.

DESIGN FEATURES

Our house and landscape were designed at the same time and as part of the same process. The original concept plan and the size and proportions of the building were not initially limited by the property boundaries and setbacks, but rather by ensuring there would be adequate garden spaces surrounding it.

Firstly, we allowed for a generous north-facing garden adjacent to the open-planned living area. The large sliding glass doors, which play such an important role allowing warming winter sun into the house, open onto an extensive deck to provide a seamless transition between inside and outdoor living spaces. Here, we have an outdoor area with sink and barbeque and a large outdoor table where we often eat our meals during summer. This set-up makes it easy to prepare and serve meals and keeps cooking heat outside. Sliding glass doors also connect the kids' playroom (a future study) onto the deck. From here they can come and go to the garden, or at least see plenty of greenery if they're playing inside when it's too hot outside or rainy. The tracks for the sliding doors are recessed and the indoor floor level matches the deck so that there are no trip hazards.

Kids' play is a key theme of the back garden in this phase of our lives. There's a built-in trampoline, a large free-form sandpit and climbing logs, all intended to look natural and age gracefully. There's a small patch of lawn that is just big enough for games, but not too big so as to be a pain to manage. It also provides a welcome, cool and lush space in an otherwise low water-use garden. Kids of course grow up, and the way the space is used will change. As part of our design, we've anticipated this

and have a transition plan in mind for how this part of the garden will adapt. The trampoline will eventually go to make room for a wood-fired oven crafted from local stone, and the sandpit will be transformed into a densely planted feature garden bed. The climbing logs and stumps will be retained as habitat features.

A small courtyard has been created in front of the master bedroom, with a fire pit and seating, as well as an outdoor shower discretely tucked to one side. Deciduous shade trees keep this area cool in summer. In winter, it acts like a sun trap and is a perfect place to sit when the weather is fine. The courtyard can be accessed directly from the bedroom via large sliding doors, either for a shower or just to go directly outside in the morning.

> We also took great care to ensure that greenery can be seen from every window in the house

We also took great care to ensure that greenery can be seen from every window in the house. For the north-facing windows, this was straightforward as they all look directly onto the garden. The windows on the southern rooms were more challenging due to the limited space. Here, we created narrow garden beds and planted vines that have now established up the walls, fence and trellises to create a lovely blanket of green. Not only does it improve the view, but it also reduces glare and radiant heat bouncing off the vertical surfaces onto the windows in summer.

Designing the block in collaboration with my sister-in-law (in the front house) has enabled us to make the most of adjoining spaces, including the driveway and space adjacent to the adjoining property boundaries. The backyard of the front house and the front yard of the back house combine to form an area that we use to grow vegetables and keep chickens, and where we have our shared composting bins, greenhouse and sheds. The area is not commonly owned; we just decided not to put a fence up and designed the space in such a way that it can be shared. The various elements have been carefully set out so that a property boundary fence can be installed in the future without anything having to be moved. Not that we see that ever happening. Keeping things practical, we set aside separate clothes drying spaces (by the laundry of each house) and also have separate east-facing carports. The rear house carport assists with providing morning summer sun protection to the building. In the front house, this function is fulfilled by a veranda.

The backyard of the front house and the front yard of the back house combine to form an area that we use to grow vegetables and keep chickens, and where we have our shared composting bins, greenhouse and sheds

We also co-designed the front garden of the front house and street verge (in accordance with local council guidelines) as part of the whole property. The required street frontage setback for the front house is dedicated to native plantings in a contemporary style that also includes a fire pit and log seating for small gatherings, providing a good way to engage with neighbours and the local community. There is also a dampland habitat feature planted with local 'winter-wet depression' suited species fed by rainfall run-off from the carport. Native plantings extend onto the verge, creating a sense of cohesion in the design.

A small courtyard area outside the master bedroom includes a fire pit and informal seating.

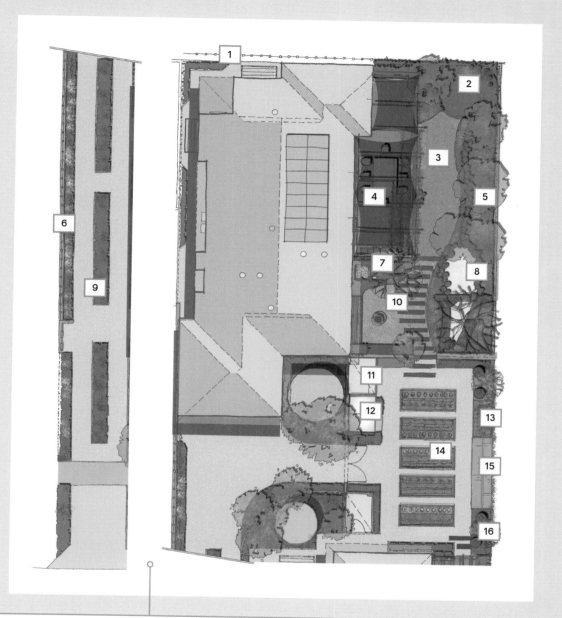

The landscape at Josh's house has been designed to support multiple sustainability outcomes, including energy efficiency, water efficiency, waste reduction, biodiversity and food production, as well as providing lifestyle benefits.

1. Clothesline
2. Trampoline
3. Lawn
4. Outdoor living area
5. Edible landscaping including fruit trees and herbs
6. Trellised fruit trees along driveway
7. Outdoor shower
8. Sandpit and climbing logs
9. Permeable surfaces including gravel and groundcovers
10. Fire pit and seating area
11. Shed
12. Nursery
13. Compost bays
14. Vegetable beds
15. Chicken pen
16. Compost bins

The garden has been designed for the whole family, with outdoor living areas, play spaces and quiet nooks. It's cooling and filled with food.

SHADING
AND AIRFLOW

Seasonal shading to complement the solar passive features of the house was one of the main considerations in the landscape design. Shade sails, along with deciduous trees and vines, have been used to ensure shade is provided when needed without obstructing winter solar gain. Likewise, careful consideration was given to the placement of structures to ensure good breeze flows across the property, particularly into the buildings.

Shade sails can be set up and taken down at exactly the right time

We selected shade sails as the main summer shading device for the outdoor deck and northern windows because they can be set up and taken down at exactly the right time. I mulled over lots of different options here, including operable louvres, retractable awnings and deciduous plants, but finally settled on custom-designed shade sails as a practical, durable and relatively cost-effective solution. The roof line that runs along the northern side of the house has no eave above the living room and playroom/study windows to allow deep light penetration into the building during winter. Having a physical shading structure that can be set up in mid-spring when the timing and temperature is right is an easy way to ensure the building doesn't overheat. Relying on plants alone to do this important job was too risky.

The shade sails work as part of an engineer-approved pergola structure that is attached to the house. One side

of the sails are securely fixed to the roof structure above the gutter line and the other is fixed to the pergola. They sit high so as not to make the deck area feel cramped. Originally, I would put up and take down the shade sails myself with each change of season. It was a clumsy process that would take a couple of hours between our place and Lisa's next door. We've since discovered that, for a small fee, the company that made and installed them will set them up and take them down. It takes them less than 30 minutes to do both houses. When the sails aren't in use, we store them out of the way.

We've also planted a grapevine on the northern edge of the pergola to provide some additional summer shade, as well as fruit. The variety is 'Perlette', a sweet, white, seedless type. Being deciduous, it loses its leaves over the winter months and we prune it back once a year to keep it tidy and ensure good fruit production. In front of the playroom and master bedroom, we've planted deciduous trees including *Gleditsia triacanthos* 'Sunburst' (honey locust) and *Lagerstroemia indica* x *fauriei* 'Natchez' (crepe myrtle) to provide additional summer shading to the house and garden. These trees were carefully selected based on their habits, maximum size and timing of leaf fall, as well as their attractive appearance.

Our landscape design has also taken into consideration the prevailing winds. We rely on the cool night-time sea breeze – very reliable in Perth – to pass through the house in summer to keep it comfortable, so the main external breezeways to the windows have been kept

clear. This was one of the main reasons that we didn't include an internal fence on the southern side of the front house – it would have been a major obstruction to the prevailing cooling summer breeze from entering the home. An additional benefit is that the arrival to our house down the driveway feels more spacious, and we have more room for growing plants in plenty of light rather than dealing with awkward shade from fences.

The other predominant wind where we live is the hot, dry easterly, which occurs in the morning in summer. It's notorious for drying out soil and plants and is generally uncomfortable. The native vegetation out on the verge and front yard is best placed to cope with these conditions, whereas we've positioned the more delicate plantings that require a protected microclimate by buildings and structures where they are sheltered. This helps to reduce irrigation requirements and improves plant success.

ABOVE: Shade sails cover the deck during summer and are taken down in winter to let light into the house.
BELOW: Grape vines provide additional shade to the deck – and fruit.

TOP LEFT: Locally sourced limestone rubble has been used to fill gabion walls.
TOP RIGHT: Salvaged untreated hardwood sleepers have been used for path steppers.
BOTTOM LEFT: Salvaged logs from removed urban landscape trees have been used for play elements.
BOTTOM RIGHT: An old truck brake drum and plough disc have been used as a fire pit.

MATERIALS

The materials used in landscape construction have an environmental impact, just as those used in house building, and the same principles apply to making more sustainable choices. Essentially, we prioritised selecting salvaged materials such as timber, locally sourced material such as limestone, and built things to be durable.

The process of design and material selection happened concurrently. Our concept plan identified key elements such as decking and pergola, but the detail of the structures, including dimensions and finish, were informed by the availability of suitable materials, particularly what was available from salvage yards. This approach is also a good way to keep costs down. By being a bit flexible with the design, we were able to respond to available materials. Unfortunately, not all tradespeople are prepared to work like this, especially when quoting. Taking the time to find the right people, who appreciate the value of working with salvaged materials, is worth the effort. If you opt for new timber for structures such as decking, pergolas and other uses, make sure it is FSC certified (au.fsc.org/en-au) as an indication that it is ethically sourced.

Choosing to use salvaged materials needn't come at the expense of aesthetics. In fact, salvaged and locally sourced materials tend to give an inherent sympathy to an area. Repetition of materials is another technique that helps unify a design. In our garden, several combinations of materials and construction styles are repeated throughout the property, such as gabion walls made from galvanised steel mesh filled with limestone rubble, which have been used for a range of purposes, from the letterbox to a fire pit plinth, through to retaining and screening walls. In a similar way, salvaged hardwood timber (jarrah) planks have been used for structures including trellises, screens and the chook pen.

Salvaged logs are another feature material of our garden, sourced from the same salvage yard as the cut timbers. Logs like these typically come from landscape trees that are being removed rather than sourced from the bush. Previously, they were chipped into mulch when cleared but they are now becoming increasingly popular as nature play items in parks and playgrounds. These were incorporated to introduce an air of informality and natural character, as well as acting as play elements and habitat features. The effort to source and install these items was well worth it.

The use of concrete has been limited to the carport and laundry patio surface, plus post and retaining wall strip footings. We haven't used any modular paving. Instead, the surface treatments for the outdoor areas are made from either timber deck or gravel, and paths are either gravel or pine-bark fines. In a few spots, paving steppers have been installed to provide definition to the mulched path lines. Here we used pieces of broken concrete footpath slab grouted together in a 'crazy paving' style. These and other second-hand paving materials and bricks are just about an inexhaustible resource to make the most of – normally for free. Garden bed edging is made from salvaged jarrah (which is naturally durable and termite resistant) where straight lines were desired, and repurposed machinery belts for curved sections.

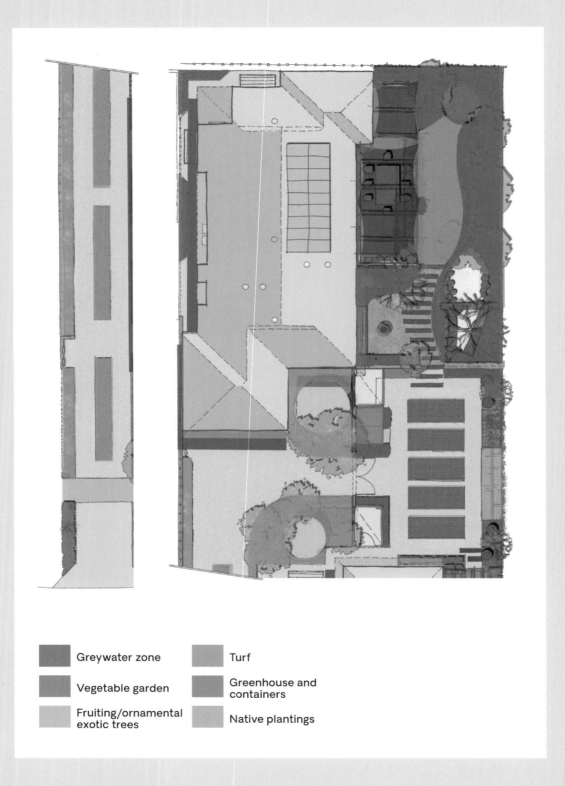

Greywater zone

Turf

Vegetable garden

Greenhouse and containers

Fruiting/ornamental exotic trees

Native plantings

WATER CONSERVATION

Our home and garden have incorporated the principles of water-sensitive design. Water is valued and utilised in all its forms, including rainwater, greywater, groundwater and mains water. The various sources are captured and recycled and applied as efficiently as possible. Chapter 6 describes the water systems that are in place at our property, including how the landscape is designed to capture and infiltrate stormwater to recharge soil moisture and the underlying aquifer, and how we use greywater in the garden as well as bore water for irrigation. Here, the design and management strategies practised to use water in the landscape efficiently and effectively are described.

Hydrozoning

Hydrozoning involves grouping plants based on their common water requirements. In this way, each hydrozone can be serviced by a separate irrigation station (or multiple stations depending on size) so that watering can be tailored. For example, native plants have very different water needs to lawn, fruit trees and vegetables, so it makes sense to service them separately. Importantly, each irrigation station, corresponding to a particular hydrozone, should use an irrigation emitter that is best suited to the type of plants being grown. For example, in our garden, sprinklers are used on the lawn, dripline irrigation is used on garden beds and spray stakes are used for container growing. By ensuring that the same emitter type is used in a zone, and provided the emitters are distributed to provide uniform watering across a zone, it is possible to accurately set an irrigation run time to water a particular plant group without under- or over-watering.

Each hydrozone can be serviced by a separate irrigation station so that watering can be tailored

---

We have the following hydrozones and irrigation emitter types:

- **Vegetable Garden**: Irrigated with groundwater using substrata dripline.

- **Fruiting and Ornamental Exotic Trees**: Irrigated with groundwater using substrata dripline.

- **Turf**: Irrigated with groundwater using rotary sprinklers.

- **Containers**: Irrigated with groundwater using spray stakes.

- **Greenhouse**: Irrigated with groundwater using misting sprinklers.

- **Perennial Plantings:** Includes a mix of herbs, shrubs, small fruit trees and vines; irrigated with greywater (with top-up capability using groundwater) using substrata dripline.

- **Native Plantings**: Irrigated with groundwater (for establishment and dry periods only) using substrata dripline.

There is a deliberate correlation between the water requirements of the hydrozones and their size, in that the largest zone (native plants) requires the least water and the high water–use zones are kept small and intensive. Planted areas requiring irrigation are evenly balanced with areas of decking, gravel and mulch pathways that don't need water. Importantly, these areas are shaded so as not to create hot spaces, and they are bordered by plantings to create a perception of lushness.

Soil Conditioning

Soil conditioners have been used to improve the water-holding capacity of the sandy soil of the site. Generous amounts of compost were initially applied to garden beds to increase the organic matter content. This approach will benefit all soils, including clay, where it helps improve structure. In all soil types it will boost microbial activity. At our place, we also added bentonite clay to the vegetable garden and fruit tree areas to further improve water and nutrient retention for these hungry plants. All areas are regularly mulched to keep plant roots and soil life cool, retain moisture

and suppress weeds. In most areas, coarse pine bark mulch with irregular particle sizes was used as it allows rain and air to pass through and it is less likely to blow away. Pine bark mulch is also long lasting. Lupin mulch, which is made from the by-product of local lupin crops, has been applied to the productive areas, including the vegetable beds and fruit trees, where it is an excellent source of organic matter for building up soil and providing nutrients for hungry plants. Lupin mulch breaks down quickly so needs to be topped up regularly and is best for protected areas. Other suitable mulches for these types of plants and protected productive areas include lucerne, pea hay and sugarcane mulch. As always, it makes sense to use products that can be sourced locally.

Pelletised poultry manure and rock mineral–based trace elements are applied to productive and exotic ornamental plantings on a seasonal basis, and homemade compost is applied to continually improve the soil. The vegetables and fruit trees receive regular applications of liquid kelp and fish emulsion. The native garden beds don't receive regular fertilising now that they are established.

TOP: Heavy droplet rotating sprinklers are used for the turf hydrozone.
BOTTOM LEFT: Compost is regularly added to the garden to improve soil moisture-holding capacity, nutrient retention and microbial activity.
BOTTOM RIGHT: Dripline is well-suited to row crops like vegetables, as well as densely planted shrub beds.

HABITAT AND BIODIVERSITY

Collectively, our gardens present the greatest potential to improve the biodiversity of our cities and towns. When combined, they make up the largest land use and, in most suburbs, dwarf the land that is set aside in parks and reserves. Our gardens also play a vital role in connecting populations of animals that need to be able to move and breed to ensure they can survive and adapt to a changing climate. For many species, if they remain isolated, they risk dying out. The opportunities to provide habitat at home are significant. There are personal benefits too. Seeing and hearing nature is good for us, and often birds and insects help our gardens thrive through pollination and natural pest control.

There are some simple things that can be done to improve the habitat value of a garden – incorporating a range of native plants (which provide nesting opportunities and food for birds and native insects), reducing paved areas and having areas of mulch and natural leaf litter (which support insects and reptiles) and foraging ground for birds. Incorporating structures such as rock walls that provide shelter and basking places for lizards and skinks will add value, as will features such as ponds, birdbaths and nesting boxes.

At our house, we've incorporated habitat features throughout the property, with some being more obvious than others. The gabion walls, for example, are teeming with skinks, and we also regularly spot them basking on the deck, where they can quickly dart between the gaps in the boards when startled. Honeyeaters of various

Flowering ornamental plants are great for attracting pollinating insects which will also pollinate fruit trees.

sorts visit the garden to feed on flowers in the backyard first thing in the morning. Most plant species in this part of the garden aren't native, but this doesn't bother them; they'll happily feed on salvias, aloes and many others, provided there's nectar to be had. Willy wagtails come into the same part of the garden to forage for insects, and we see them picking black house spiders straight off the webs made around our window frames. Birds of all sorts come to drink and bathe at the birdbaths. We have two – a large one and a small one, separated so the big birds don't bully the little ones out of the way.

The garden is also teeming with beneficial insects including lacewings, hoverflies and ladybirds. The

juveniles of all three species predate on common sap-sucking pest insects such as aphids and scale. We have plenty of butterflies too, helping with pollination and delighting the kids, and of course plenty of bees – both native species and honey bees. All we have to do to keep these species inhabiting our garden is grow a diverse variety of flowers and not use toxic pesticides.

We have frogs (*Litoria moorei*) in a small pond planted with edible species such as Lebanese cress, water chestnut and green taro. The pond also attracts dragonflies and is filled with local freshwater pygmy perch (*Nannoperca vittata*) to keep mosquito larvae at bay. We find frogs all over the garden at night, searching for insects to eat and probably snails too.

All this biological activity contributes toward urban biodiversity. From healthy soil filled with microbes and invertebrates, to nooks and crannies for beetles, spiders and reptiles, to bird-attracting plants and ponds that support fish and frogs, it's all important and it all adds up.

TOP LEFT: Pardalote nesting box.
MIDDLE LEFT: Skink sunning on the compost bay.
BOTTOM LEFT: Climbing logs make great habitat features.
TOP RIGHT: A small pond supports fish, frogs and aquatic insects.
BOTTOM RIGHT: Everlastings put on a showy display and are great for attracting beneficial insects.
BOTTOM FAR RIGHT: A feature post with old borer holes acts as an insect hotel for native bees.

Winter veggie harvest including cabbage, potatoes, lettuce, silbverbeet and Asian greens.

FOOD PRODUCTION AND COMPOSTING

Food production is an important element of our garden. The veggie garden is probably the most obvious feature, made up of five beds measuring 3 m by 1.5 m each, totalling just over 20 m² all up. The width of the beds makes them easy to manage as it is comfortable to reach in without over-extending. Having multiple beds allows us to rotate crops each season to reduce the likelihood of pest and disease issues. We harvest something from the veggie garden most days and regularly share and preserve produce.

We harvest something from the veggie garden most days and regularly share and preserve produce

---

This kitchen garden area also includes the chicken pen, a neat 6 m² structure where we keep four chickens that provide enough eggs for both households most weeks of the year. Around the perimeters of the kitchen garden are trellised fruit trees and vines, including fig, plum, grape and passionfruit, as well as dwarf and standard varieties, including nashi pear, apple, pear, strawberry guava and peach. At ground level, there is rhubarb, thornless blackberry and all sorts of flowers and culinary herbs.

This is also the place where we deal with most of our household organic waste for recycling back into the garden. Good-quality scraps go straight to the chooks, which convert the material into eggs and manure. Other kitchen scraps go into one of four cone-type compost bins that are used in rotation. Once one is full, we start on the next one. By the time we fill up the second and the third, the first one is ready for use, and around and around it goes. The bins are buried slightly (around 150 mm) to prevent rodents and cockroaches getting in, and they are located alongside fruit trees, which benefit from the rich compost at the base. We also have two large compost bays, each with an internal cubic capacity of 1.25 m³, and these are used to process the green waste generated from the garden such as crop trash, grass clippings and prunings. We also compost weeds. Where possible, we pull these up and add them to the pile before they set seed. Larger pieces of wood, which may come from occasional pruning of the trees, are used in the fire pit, and the ash goes into the bays. We generate all the compost we need from these systems and no longer need to buy any.

The kitchen garden area also includes a greenhouse for raising plants, a potting bench for propagation and a small garden shed. Everything is carefully laid out, including taps and even a washdown sink that can be set up over the compost bays to make it easy to get on with the task of growing food.

The driveway also has a number of trellised fruit trees that were planted in a narrow bed along the fence line, including Chinese date, Indian tree guava, olive, dwarf black mulberry, apricot, apple and pear. The trees do well despite the narrow bed because their roots can extend out under the gravel that forms the driveway,

ABOVE & LEFT: The chicken pen has been designed to make collecting the eggs easy.
TOP RIGHT: The Leghorn–New Hampshire cross hens are good layers and have a good temperament for urban gardens.
BOTTOM RIGHT: The shared veggie garden with summer crops underway, including cucumber, corn, tomatoes and beans.

where they can search for soil moisture and get plenty of air. In between the trees are understorey plantings of flowering companion plants as well as globe artichokes, shallots and other herbs.

Our back garden also includes productive species, which are mixed in with ornamental plants to create a diverse edible landscape. Here, we've planted handsome edible trees, including pomegranate, quince and assorted citrus, which look good as well as being highly productive. There's also lots of culinary herbs and picking greens, both in the ground and in containers, for easy access from the kitchen. Another area includes bananas, which thrive on greywater and provide a lush look in summer and beautiful fruit. When the bananas come on, we have so many that we freeze them for smoothies and dry them for chewy sweet snacks.

BELOW: Composting cones are partially buried to deter rodents and are located under fruit trees (nashi pear) to provide a source of nutrients.
RIGHT: A small greenhouse is used to raise plants for the garden.

CHAPTER 8

PERFORMANCE VERIFICATION & MONITORING

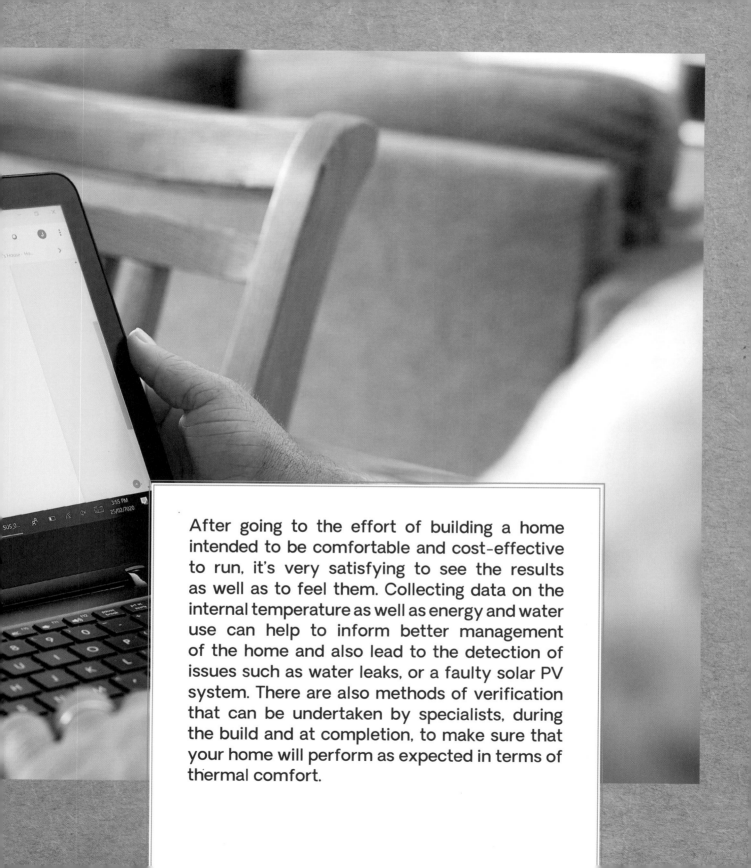

After going to the effort of building a home intended to be comfortable and cost-effective to run, it's very satisfying to see the results as well as to feel them. Collecting data on the internal temperature as well as energy and water use can help to inform better management of the home and also lead to the detection of issues such as water leaks, or a faulty solar PV system. There are also methods of verification that can be undertaken by specialists, during the build and at completion, to make sure that your home will perform as expected in terms of thermal comfort.

AIRTIGHTNESS TEST

There is growing industry and consumer attention on the airtightness of buildings and how this impacts the heating and cooling requirements of a house. In cool climates, air leakage from poorly sealed houses is particularly problematic, leading to increased heating costs as well as condensation and mould issues within walls and other parts of the building fabric. Heat loss through uncontrolled air leakage is particularly relevant to houses built using lightweight materials because they lack the thermal mass to retain heat and stabilise the temperature. Poor airtightness also correlates to greater ingress of dust, insects and smoke.

Heat loss through uncontrolled air leakage is particularly relevant to houses built using lightweight materials as they lack the thermal mass to retain heat and stabilise the temperature

---

Airtightness is assessed by conducting a blower door test. The process involves temporarily fitting an adjustable panel tightly inside an exterior door frame and closing all other windows and doors. A fan is switched on and the volume of air blown into the building at 50 pascals (Pa) is recorded. Results are typically presented as Air Changes per Hour (ACH50), which describes the number of times the volume of air inside the building is replaced at 50 Pa of pressure. Results in the range of 3.5 to 7 ACH50 are considered good. Studies have shown that the airtightness of new Australian homes averages around 15 ACH50, so there's serious room for improvement.

A blower door test costs around $500. Currently, there is no requirement at either a national or state level to have building airtightness tested; however, a number of commercial operators offer it as a service. When we built our house in 2013, there were no blower door test units available in Perth. Now there are several companies that provide the service, and many more in other states.

Rather than waiting until your home is completed to test for airtightness – at which point fixing some of the causes can be difficult – it is better to check at key points in the construction process to identify issues that may result in air leakage. This includes visual inspections at wall framings and window fittings where gaps can be caulked; after plastering to ensure all penetrations are properly sealed; and at completion where final things such as door seals are checked. The process is normally undertaken by a contractor or the building designer and should be agreed upon with your builder prior to finalising the building contract so that expectations are clear.

ABOVE RIGHT: A thermal imaging camera can be used to identify weak points such as thermal bridging or gaps in insulation.

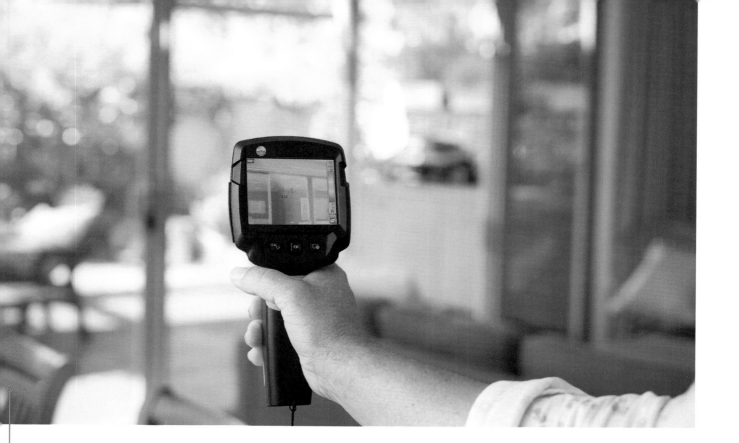

THERMOGRAPHY TEST

Another useful verification method for quality control is thermal imaging using a camera that measures the infrared radiation being emitted by a surface. The results are presented across a colour spectrum with light colours representing heat and darker colours representing cooler surfaces. Thermal imagery can be used to identify air leaks, which can then be sealed, as well as to identify areas of missing insulation which will become weak points in terms of heat loss and heat gain between the house and the external environment. Just like with the air leakage test, it's best to identify issues with poor or insufficient insulation installation

early, especially wall insulation and insulation that is installed in hard-to-access parts of the ceiling. Often, the technician who is engaged to check for potential air leakage issues during the building process will also check the insulation, and these services are not particularly expensive. Once again, communicate your expectations early with your builder. Proactive builders who are committed to a good outcome will be agreeable and will likely be able to recommend suitable contractors to provide the service, with some now offering it as a part of their package. Otherwise, an online search will soon provide you with options.

PERFORMANCE MONITORING

Collecting operational data such as temperature readings, energy and water use is the definitive way to assess the performance of your home. The simplest and most cost-effective way to do this is to get single-channel wireless devices to collect individual sets of data. For example, a single point temperature sensor with a data logger can be used to record the temperature of a room at set time periods and provide it on a display for immediate viewing, and also store the information for later use to observe trends.

Monitoring your energy use is easy too. Most solar inverters come with basic monitoring capability, with the information accessible from an app. It's worth noting that the standard function of these will typically only provide data on solar energy generated and exported. Additional metering devices are required to capture energy imports to have a complete understanding of your energy consumption and degree of self-supply. This can be obtained from your electricity bill of course, but having this information in real-time, or near real-time, is much more powerful for the purpose of providing feedback on household energy use and to inform energy-saving behaviour.

There are also simple water monitoring devices that can be connected to your water meter to read a signal and transmit it to a display screen inside the home. Like the energy meter, this can provide useful information to help reduce water use. Systems that collect data from multiple channels – such as different electrical loads, as well as water – are available with user-friendly displays, and as technology is advancing all the time, it means they are becoming cheaper and more common. This technology is well established in the commercial sector and it is gradually filtering down to the residential market.

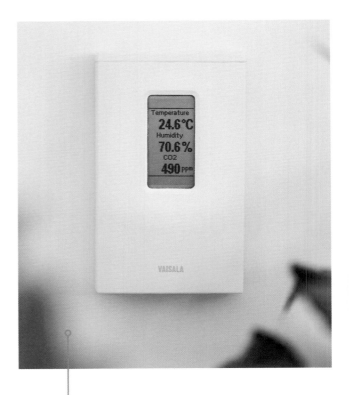

ABOVE: This wall-mounted sensor at Josh's house monitors and displays internal temperature, relative humidity and carbon dioxide levels.
RIGHT: The electrical circuit board at Josh's house includes energy meters for every circuit to enable detailed research on energy use.

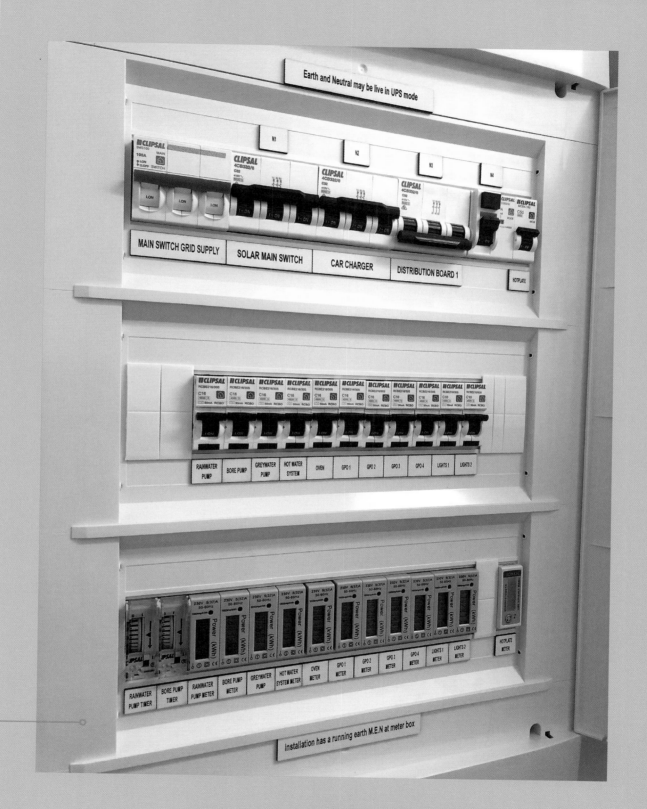

Earth and Neutral may be live in UPS mode

MAIN SWITCH GRID SUPPLY   SOLAR MAIN SWITCH   CAR CHARGER   DISTRIBUTION BOARD 1   HOTPLATE

RAINWATER PUMP   BORE PUMP   GREYWATER PUMP   HOT WATER SYSTEM   OVEN   GPO 1   GPO 2   GPO 3   GPO 4   LIGHTS 1   LIGHTS 2

RAINWATER PUMP TIMER   BORE PUMP TIMER   RAINWATER PUMP METER   BORE PUMP METER   GREYWATER PUMP   HOT WATER SYSTEM METER   OVEN METER   GPO 1 METER   GPO 2 METER   GPO 3 METER   GPO 4 METER   LIGHTS 1 METER   LIGHTS 2 METER   HOTPLATE METER

Installation has a running earth M.E.N at meter box

GREENSMART TABLE

The following tables demonstrate how Josh's house addressed the HIA GreenSmart objectives during the design and construction process. As outlined on page 30, the GreenSmart categories include Energy Management, Water Management, Material Selection, Indoor Air Quality Management, Universal Design, Site Management and Resource-Efficient Practice. The tables present a series of objectives under each category, example design features that are required to meet the objectives, and the specific initiative employed at Josh's house to achieve these.

Energy Management

GREENSMART OBJECTIVES: THE HOME MUST	EXAMPLE DESIGN FEATURES THAT CLARIFY THE GREENSMART OBJECTIVES	OUR HOUSE
Achieve a minimum thermal performance rating	Does the house achieve a minimum 6-star (or equivalent) thermal performance rating?	10-star NatHERS rating – rated by a certified assessor
Be designed to take advantage of natural lighting and passive solar heating throughout the year (southern climates zones)	Has the house been designed to achieve the best possible orientation for living areas to control and benefit from solar access?	House is orientated on an east–west axis with main living areas and large windows to the northern side
Limit solar absorption through glazing during summer and loss during winter	Has solar absorption on east and west elevations been minimised and northern elevation been managed appropriately through limited glazing, glazing treatment or installation of eaves/shading devices?	No glazing on the west elevation; one window on the east elevation, shaded by the carport; low-e glazing installed Detail: Single Low-e (most windows): U-value 4.70; Solar Heat Gain Coefficient (SHGC) 0.63. Double Glazing: U-value 4.27; Solar Heat Gain Coefficient (SHGC) 0.67
Be designed to take advantage of prevailing breezes where they exist, e.g. coastal or sloping sites and natural ventilation	Has the house been designed with windows and openings that can capture prevailing breezes and assist in desired air circulation?	Cross ventilation and local climate are fundamental to the design
Incorporate room zoning to reduce the areas required to be artificially heated or cooled	Does the home design include doors, walls or other features that allow groups of rooms to be closed off to create smaller spaces for heating and cooling? Min. two zones required.	Bedroom wing can be closed off from main living area; activity room can be closed off from main living area
Incorporate building sealing control to reduce heat transfer through openings	Have draught seals been placed around windows and external doors?	Air-conditioning rated seals to external doors and windows
Reduce greenhouse gas emissions from hot-water systems	Will the hot-water system be minimum 5-star or equivalent solar system? (For example, gas boosted SHW, gas 5-star instantaneous, gas 5-star storage and electric heat pump)	Original: 300 L gas-boosted solar hot-water system 2018 Upgrade: Changed to a heat pump system, timed to operate during the day to take advantage of a larger PV system also installed; gas cooktop changed to induction so that gas could be disconnected Detail: Bosch 270 L heat pump, timed for daytime heating

GREENSMART OBJECTIVES: THE HOME MUST	EXAMPLE DESIGN FEATURES THAT CLARIFY THE GREENSMART OBJECTIVES	OUR HOUSE
Reduce energy consumption from traditional lighting fixtures	Does the design include the use of compact fluorescent light bulbs, fluorescent tubes, LED or similar energy-efficient lighting in at least 80% of the light fixtures?	Dimmable LED downlights in the bedrooms and living areas (kitchen, dining, living room and activity room). compact fluorescent globes in occasional-use areas (bathroom, laundry, toilet and hallway)
Reduce reliance on drying with appliances	Will the home be provided with a clothesline which receives solar access? (For display homes an area can be nominated)	Clothesline fixed to western wall of house, with an additional area allowed for on the south elevations
Educate the occupants on their energy consumption patterns	Will an energy usage meter be installed and located in a living area or high trafficked area?	Comprehensive monitoring system as part of living lab research project that centres on the home Note: Monitoring data can be seen live online at joshshouse.com.au
Reduce demand on traditional energy sources	Will the home include a minimum 1 kWp renewable energy system?	Original: 3kW photovoltaic solar array and 2.5 kW inverter 2018 Upgrade: Replaced with new high-performance PV system; old system reused elsewhere; battery system upgraded with new 10 kWh system, replacing a system installed in 2015; old battery reused elsewhere Detail: 6.4 kWp array of SunPower modules on a 5 kWp Fronius Hybrid inverter (able to deliver DC to the new battery storage system also upgraded in 2018)
Reduce the potential heat transfer around window frames	Are the windows thermally efficient, do they incorporate thermally efficient frame design (i.e. thermally broken, timber, uPVC or fibreglass frames)?	One double glazed, thermally broken window in the kitchen Other frames are powder-coated aluminium as suited to the climate zone and design; well fitted to achieve good building sealing and reduce draughts
Incorporate the ability to control the loss of heated or cooled air movement to the outside	Is there a door between the entrance foyer and adjoining rooms allowing the creation of an airlock?	Daytime living areas are isolated from the night zones via the passageway
Incorporate energy-efficient household appliances	Will the fixed appliances installed in the home achieve an energy rating within 1 star of maximum available?	Fridge, dishwasher and washing machine all 4-star under the Energy Rating label scheme (4.5-stars typically being the highest at the time)
Promote energy-efficient heating and cooling systems	Where planned to be installed, the artificial heating and/or cooling systems will achieve maximum energy efficiency rating that is currently available on the market. Will ceiling fans be installed in living areas and bedrooms?	No heating or cooling system installed Reversible ceiling fans installed in living rooms and bedrooms

Energy Management (continued)

GREENSMART OBJECTIVES: THE HOME MUST	EXAMPLE DESIGN FEATURES THAT CLARIFY THE GREENSMART OBJECTIVES	OUR HOUSE
Reduce internal heat transfer through windows and openings	Will thermally backed (energy-efficient) window coverings or window pelmets be fitted in the habitable rooms and bedrooms?	Window pelmets and thermally backed window coverings installed
Reduce external heat transfer through windows and openings	Have operable blinds or awnings been incorporated to protect northern- and western-facing windows from summer sun?	No western windows; removable shade sail awning to north-facing windows of open-plan living areas
Incorporate skylights as a means of ventilation and natural lighting	Where skylights are provided, are they openable, dimmable or shadable?	Solartube skylight installed in hallway and walk-in robe
Incorporate thermal mass construction as appropriate for the climate conditions	Have materials with thermal mass been internally utilised within the design to provide passive heating and cooling to the home?	North-facing external walls are cavity brickwork; floor is sealed concrete; internal walls are brickwork; selected walls are reverse brick veneer
Incorporate lightweight construction as appropriate for the climate conditions	Have lightweight external cladding materials been used where appropriate?	Selected walls are reverse brick veneer (lightweight cladding externally with single-leaf brick internal wall) and timber framed with cladding as appropriate to the climate zone and design
Improve building envelope thermal performance – walls	Has insulation been added to walls to improve thermal performance?	Cavity brick, stud frame and reverse brick veneer fitted with Permicav. Achieves R2.0
Improve building envelope thermal performance – ceilings	Has insulation been added to ceilings to improve thermal performance?	Bulk insulation (batts) on plaster ceiling. Downlight penetrations hooded. Achieves R4.0
Improve building envelope thermal performance – roof	Has insulation been added to the roof to improve thermal performance?	Foil-backed insulation under steel roof on wooden frame; roof is Colorbond 'Cream' colour ('Light', SAV < 0.475) Framing timber is white-ant treated (Light Organic Solvent Preservative, LOSP, for reduced impact) plantation pine; achieves R1.5 **Note:** Roof and ceiling performance combine to achieve above R5.5 for roof construction

Water Management

GREENSMART OBJECTIVES: THE HOME MUST	EXAMPLE DESIGN FEATURES THAT CLARIFY THE GREENSMART OBJECTIVES	OUR HOUSE
Reduce potable water consumption in toilets	Will all toilets have a minimum 4-star WELS rating (where plumbing codes support their use)?	Caroma close-coupled toilet suite (4-star) Caroma toilet suite with integrated hand basin (5-star)
Reduce potable water consumption in showers	Will all showers be fitted with a minimum 3-star WELS-rated showerhead?	Caroma shower heads (3-stars)
Limit potable water consumption in basins and sinks	Will all hand basins and sinks be fitted with minimum 4-star rated tapware?	Caroma sink mixer (4-star) Trident basin tap set (5-star)
Use efficient appliances	Will dishwasher and washing machine come with high WELS ratings?	Both dishwasher and washing machine quality brands with WELS 4.5-star ratings
Incorporate alternative water supplies for internal use	Will an additional alternate water supply be provided for toilets, laundries or hot water services, e.g. third pipe reticulation system, rainwater tank, treated greywater or blackwater systems (where legislation permits)?	20 kL steel rain tank with food-grade liner, collecting off 200 m² roof catchment; filtered rainwater plumbed to all internal fittings and fixtures; treatment of rainwater: two-stage filtering (20-micron then 1-micron), followed by UV disinfection (Davey Steriflo)
Incorporate alternative water supplies for external use	Will an additional alternate water supply be provided for external use, e.g. third pipe reticulation system, treated greywater or blackwater systems (where legislation permits)?	Greywater and bore water for all external water uses and irrigation Greywater uses a direct diversion system (AWWS GreyFlow PS) Bore water provides fit-for-purpose water for food production (where greywater may not be appropriate). 30 m deep bore sits under the driveway. Bore pump is a submersible Grundfos unit with variable speed drive
Provide appropriate plumbing connections to allow future treatment and reuse of wastewater	Will all wastewater drainage lines be designed to extend to the external walls before interconnecting with stormwater drainage? (concrete slab construction only)	Greywater reuse system is installed; piping is accessible for future upgrades or system changes
Reduce the need for watering of garden areas	Where gardens are included in the design, have they been designed to minimise water use and/ or to retain rainwater in the garden area?	Hydrozoned garden design Soil conditioner installed to garden beds; minimum 75 mm thick mulch to all garden beds Efficient irrigation systems for both bore water and greywater reuse All stormwater infiltrated on site, through permeable paving, soakwells or dampland drainage basins Waterwise plants make up majority of plantings, including the native verge garden

Material Selection

GREENSMART MATERIAL CATEGORIES	AIM OF MATERIAL CHOICES	OUR HOUSE
External cladding	Will the project use renewable materials, non-renewable materials that have been recycled or contain recycled content, or materials that can be recycled at the end of their life?	Face brickwork: Midland Brick (Boral) Bricks can be recycled/ reused upon demolition of structure, recyclable as an aggregate
Sub-floor construction	As above	Holcim, low carbon concrete, 30% fly ash content Recyclable as crushed concrete aggregate
Roofing material	As above	BlueScope Steel (Colorbond) Steel sheeting can be recycled/reused upon demolition of structure
Framing material	As above	LOSP pine timber-framed roof and stud wall structure: low carbon emissions material with reduced toxicity termite treatment; can be recycled/reused upon demolition of structure
Plasterboard	As above	Boral plasterboard; external surfaces composed of 100% recycled paper
Windows and doors	As above	Factory-finished aluminium window frames; aluminium fully recyclable
Construction timber	As above	Deck framing and pergola framing: repurposed local hardwood (jarrah)
Other	As above	Low emission E0 and E1 timber products for kitchen, laundry and wardrobe fit-outs Deck framing and pergola framing: repurposed local hardwood (jarrah)
Decrease the demand on non-renewable virgin resources and increase diversion of waste from landfill	As above	Genuine site waste put into skip bins for processing at recycling facility with target of 80–90% resource recovery rate Waste strategy in place specifying cabinetry and steel beams be cut and fabricated offsite. Targets set for wastage to guide procurement, including: Bricks 5% (taken to nearest $1/4$ pack); tiles 5%; concrete 3%; paving bricks 3% (taken to nearest $1/2$ pack); plasterboard 5% (ordered to length to reduce large off-cuts) Sustainably sourced timber, a renewable resource, used wherever suitable
Promote the use of physical termite barriers and termite resistant materials where possible and where required	Will physical termite management systems be installed around and within the perimeter of the home? Will the home be constructed using termite resistant materials?	Physical termite barrier (Termimesh) used Treated (low human toxicity) pine utilised in construction Recycled local hardwood (jarrah) used for hard landscaping elements and patio construction

Indoor Air Quality Management

GREENSMART OBJECTIVES: THE HOME MUST BE DESIGNED TO	EXAMPLE DESIGN FEATURES THAT CLARIFY THE GREENSMART OBJECTIVES	OUR HOUSE
Take advantage of natural and active sources of air circulation to reduce odours and allow fresh air to enter	Does the design take advantage of air circulation through natural ventilation in active rooms (kitchen, bathrooms, laundry)? Where appropriate, has the design included active (ceiling fans) and automated systems?	House designed to promote natural cross ventilation; ceiling fans installed in all habitable rooms; exhaust fans installed in bathrooms, toilets and kitchen
Reduce mould build-up in roof cavity	Have features been designed or installed to enable ventilation in the roof space to avoid mould creation, e.g. whirly birds, vents?	Western Solar SV10 solar powered vent installed to exhaust roof cavity air
Reduce exposure to formaldehyde in plywood (laminate) products	Will plywood products contain formaldehyde content of 1 mg/L or less (as per the relevant Australian standard)?	Kitchen, laundry and wardrobe fit-outs: Laminex standard E0 and E1 low formaldehyde products
Reduce exposure to formaldehyde in particleboard or fibreboard products	Will kitchen, bathroom and laundry cupboards contain formaldehyde content of 1.5 mg/L or less?	Kitchen, laundry and wardrobe fit-outs: Laminex standard E0 and E1 low formaldehyde products
Incorporate paints, finishes and varnishes that have a low volatile organic compound (VOC) content	Where paint, decorative finishes, coatings, stains or transparent finishes are used, will they achieve total VOC emissions of 0.5 mg/m^3 or less seven days from application?	Low-VOC interior paints: Wattyl Aqua Trim Gloss Enamel Wattyl I.D Luxury Low Sheen Wattyl I.D Silky Satin Wattyl I.D Ceiling White
Reduce exposure to VOC from floor coverings	Will floor coverings achieve VOC emissions of 0.5 mg/metre^2/hour or less as tested using a 24-hour protocol like ASTM D5116?	Floor paint: Dulux Luxafloor Eco2 Low Sheen (low VOC)

Universal Design

GREENSMART OBJECTIVES: THE HOME MUST HAVE	EXAMPLE DESIGN FEATURES THAT CLARIFY THE GREENSMART OBJECTIVES	OUR HOUSE
At least one level entrance into the dwelling to enable occupants to easily enter and exit the dwelling	Is there at least one covered 820 mm clear-width entry doorway into the home, with a level transition, landing and threshold and reasonable shelter from the weather, connected to the level pathway (i.e. from garage or street)?	Front door 920 mm wide; under cover; recessed entry door sill and unimpeded access through to all areas of house
Bathroom and toilet walls built to enable grab rails to be safely and economically installed	Will the wall framing in the bathroom be reinforced or of materials that allow future installation of grab rails in the shower and adjacent to the toilet or will grab rails be installed?	Brick internal walls in both bathrooms suitable for grab rails
A bathroom and shower designed for easy and independent access for all home occupants	Does the plan contain a hobless/step-free shower recess located in the corner of the bathroom to allow future installation of handrails?	Hobless shower recess; design allows for future handrail installation
Internal doors and corridors that facilitate comfortable and unimpeded movement between spaces	Will all internal doorways on the entrance levels have a minimum clear width opening of 820 mm and corridors of 1 m or wider?	870 mm internal doors throughout; corridors exceed 1 m width
Room to allow a person to open their car doors fully and easily move around the vehicle, where the parking space is part of the safe and continuous pathway	Where part of the dwelling access pathway, is the car parking space a minimum of 3.2 x 5.4 m, with an even, slip-resistant surface and level surface?	Double carport 6.6 x 6.5 m with exposed aggregate concrete floor
A ground (or entry) level toilet to support easy access for home occupants and visitors	Does the home incorporate a toilet on the same level as the level entry doorway? Is the toilet within a room with a minimum width of 900 mm and at least 1200 mm in front of the toilet pan?	Main toilet: in 2100 x 1400 mm space, 1250 mm in front of pan, doorway clearance of 870 mm

Site Management

GREENSMART OBJECTIVES: THE SITE MUST BE MANAGED TO ENSURE THAT	EXAMPLE DESIGN/CONSTRUCTION PROCESS	OUR HOUSE
Site disturbance (cut/fill/ scouring) during construction is minimised	Does the house design minimise the amount of cut and fill required to the site and the area which requires disturbance?	Small amount of fill to achieve required levels and falls across site
Stockpiles are controlled in a way that reduces material leaving the site during construction	Will stockpiles of soil, sand and other materials be placed in areas away from street gutters and drainage lines?	All spoil was managed on site and protected from rain, wind and spread by traffic
Construction waste and rubbish are not able to be blown off site during construction	Have containers been provided on site to store construction waste and litter?	Site bins provided throughout construction; regular tidy ups undertaken
Vehicles use a single access point on and off the site during construction	Will an all-weather access driveway (crushed rock or similar material) be provided from the street onto the site?	Local site sand provided suitable trafficable surface
At the completion of building work, all exposed soil is stabilised and all construction waste removed	Will the exposed areas of the site be stabilised with turf and/or plantings and cleared of debris prior to occupancy when job is finished?	All major landscaping completed prior to occupancy

Resource-Efficient Practice

GREENSMART OBJECTIVES: CONSTRUCTION SHOULD BE MANAGED TO ENSURE THAT	EXAMPLE DESIGN/CONSTRUCTION MEASURE	OUR HOUSE
Recyclable building materials (off cuts, broken or excess) are separated from general waste	Will a separate waste bin or collection area be provided on site for construction waste that can be recycled?	Recycling bins provided throughout construction; supplier recycling facility targets 80–90% recycling
Ordering of materials is integrated with the design to minimise wastage	What systems have been put in place to ensure accurate ordering procedures of materials and methods to reduce packaging?	Site measuring required for roof sheeting, cabinetry; strict guidelines met for target wastage quantities
Prefabricated construction systems are used, where appropriate, to minimise building waste during construction	Will the construction materials include use of prefabricated timber frames, roof trusses, or other fixtures such as cabinetry?	Not applicable

INDEX

Diagrams/illustrations, graphs and tables are marked *(d)*, *(g)* and *(t)*, respectively.

DR JOSH BYRNE is an environmental scientist, gardener, TV presenter, author, consultant and academic. Well known for his role as a presenter on ABC's *Gardening Australia* program, Josh is also a Research Fellow at Curtin University's School of Design and the Built Environment, where his research activities span high-performance housing, water-sensitive design and sustainable urban development. He is the author of two books on sustainable gardening and has written a number of academic book chapters, journal papers and industry guidelines relating to low-carbon living and water-sensitive design.

Josh is Director of Josh Byrne & Associates, a consulting practice integrating the fields of landscape architecture and built environment sustainability, with offices in Fremantle and Melbourne, and a portfolio of projects spanning urban development and civic space design. His approach is leadership through demonstration. He engages in projects at various scales that provide opportunities to test innovation, build capacity and share learnings with stakeholders and the broader community.

ACKNOWLEDGEMENTS

This book is the final milestone in a long series of planned activities to do with our house project, spanning the design and construction of the building, a research program, a website, tours and videos – so this seems a fitting opportunity to acknowledge the many people and organisations that I collaborated with along the way.

Firstly, to our building design partner, Griff Morris, who has been a source of inspiration and industry leadership for years. Griff's willingness to collaborate and share his knowledge and experience for the advancement of climate-sensible design is legendary. He's one of the hardest working and most selfless people I know, and this project wouldn't have been the success it is without him.

To our builder, Jim DeBaughn, who bent over backwards to help us achieve our dream home and remained open to the ideas we wanted to test and share with others.

We were also supported by a group of incredible tradespeople and craftsmen who left their mark on the project and, in doing so, have made an impact on the housing industry. I grabbed every opportunity to learn from these talented people and am the richer for it.

We were also fortunate to work with a number of industry partners. These partnerships were strategic to ensure we brought the best industry knowledge to the project, as well as creating networks to share our learnings with the industry. I am grateful to our partners for their support and input.

I was also fortunate to draw on the skills of work colleagues in the design of the house and landscape.

This extended to media and communication activities, from graphic design and publications to open house events; all of these were made possible through team work. A special mention must go to my long-term collaborator Brendan Hutchens for his role in producing the Josh's House video series, as well as my Communications Manager D'arcy Hodgkinson for overseeing a six-year campaign that just kept getting bigger.

One of the reasons for the interest in the Josh's House project is the research program developed to monitor and assess the performance of the house, and then openly share the findings. This was a unique opportunity initiated by my colleague Professor Peter Newman, who immediately saw the potential and importance of this work. It was supported by the CRC for Low Carbon Living, particularly Professor Deo Prasad, Dr Stephen White and the CRC's Board of Directors.

And now, to the book. Firstly, to Dr Kellie Maher, for her contribution in researching many aspects of this book and her role in co-designing the house. Also, to my colleague Mark Taylor, who is a subject-matter expert in the built environment and has provided me with exceptional support. To the team at Hardie Grant, especially Anna Collett, as well as copy-editor Kate Daniel and designer Emily O'Neill. To Rob Frith, who has photographed the house over the years, as well as to the other talented photographers for their contributions.

And finally, to my partner, Kellie, our children, Ollie and Caitlin, and Lisa and Grace next door. Thank you for allowing me to share our homes and garden with the world. Let's hope it makes a difference.

Published in 2020 by Hardie Grant Books, an imprint of Hardie Grant Publishing

Hardie Grant Books (Melbourne)
Building 1, 658 Church Street
Richmond, Victoria 3121

hardiegrantbooks.com

Hardie Grant Books (London)
5th & 6th Floors
52–54 Southwark Street
London SE1 1UN

 A catalogue record for this book is available from the National Library of Australia

The Sustainable House Handbook

ISBN 978 1 74379 582 8

10 9 8 7 6 5 4 3 2

Publishing Director: Pam Brewster
Project Editor: Anna Collett
Editor: Kate Daniel
Design Manager: Jessica Lowe
Designer: Emily O'Neill
Photographers: Robert Frith, Morgan Gillham, Brendan Hutchens, Josh Byrne, Joel Barbitta, Kathy Johnston, SJD Homes
Production Manager: Todd Rechner
Production Coordinator: Mietta Yans

Colour reproduction by Splitting Image Colour Studio
Printed in China by Leo Paper Products LTD.